An Anthropological History of the African Diaspora

Sherma Rismay

A Concise Survey of the African Diaspora in History,
from essays compiled for a Bachelor's Degree in
History with a minor concentration in Anthropology.

ISBN 9781984956217

Cover image from of Charlemagne first king of all of Europe, from the Coronation of the king, depicted in the Sacramentary of Charles the Bald (ca. 870) Paris, Bibliothèque nationale de France, ms. Latin 1141, A close examination of the Halos in many pieces appear to have been the impression of overgrown Afros.

The BluePrint Publishing Company.
119 Plainfield St
Hartford, CT 06112
Theblueprints.org
Theblueprintsforlife.org
shema@theblueprintsforlife.org

Empires just like Earth have been subject to rise and fall as their source of power rotated. According to Egyptian legend, Osiris was God of the night while Min was God of the day. When Osiris the God of night prevailed, the "children of the sun" as the Egyptians referred to themselves, would go to the sunken place or the underworld. They would be divided into many pieces, spread and buried throughout the world. Isis as the guardian of what had been buried, initiates the resurrection by putting all the pieces back together. Isis is the [1]queen of the south. She would prevail, to give birth to Horus, the symbol of a new generation. The sun was eclipsed around the end of the eighteenth century. At that time, a period of darkness initiated the dream of a new world. Today [2]the clock is ticking and *we are* [3]"on the pulse of morning, now counting" mins, before our dead rise and a new day begins.

---

[1] Revelation 12

[2] Kanye West "Power"

[3] Maya Angelo

TABLE OF CONTENTS

Preface

This anthropological construction of African diasporic history, asks new questions, challenges old assumptions and conducts a more scientific inquisition into historical events. It reconstructs particular eras through the eyes of the observer, but with the objectivity of a modern scientist. This methodology challenges the cultural paradigm of earlier researchers to dissect their interpretations from the facts. This essentially turns the lens on the author, to examine who is telling the story, their biases as well as the intent of their production. This is different from simply quoting or restating a past idea or perception. It is what I have referred to as "Transcribed Archeology," the study of literature or art (including music, drawings and all transcribed forms of cultural expression) as artifacts. Then anchoring these artifacts within the context of the generation which produced them. The intangible social elements expressed through popular art, speaks to a consensus of a community to expose the friction or social distinctions.

Statements like: "in 1620 a ship of 20 Negroes was brought to Virginia," can be reevaluated by separating what is factual, from what is phrased to affect the interpretation of the fact. What is known, is that 20 Africans arrived in Virginia in 1621, whether brought, carried or immigrated freely, is the intent of this research. Black American History, usually starts with Blacks being chained and carried across the ocean, on sea voyages which lasted several weeks, to finally be enslaved in the Americas. The most effective tool used in this imagery is a narrowed concentration on one aspect of the story. The image of this physically dominant man, degenerated and chained, conjures up such an impressive sense of powerlessness, which resonates with the current state of Black America, that it tends to legitimize this story. Such a journey, especially then, was like going to the moon and even today, would require a substantial amount of wealth. Yet the identity of the traders and the enterprise which required the transplantation of millions of Black people, is almost never connected to the philanthropists. Slavery happened, this is an undeniable fact, but when placed in the context of a global society, the reasoning which has been provided and the circumstances under which slavery did take place, are the elements of the story now in question. This study is only a snippet of an extensive undertaking, ahead of a few more years of research and quilting, which the final project will undoubtedly require. This concise version, has been submitted in response to a wave of events, which have placed a great urgency to release this project in its infant state. Although unfinished, the object of the final edition, which is to relate history as one stream of continuous and interconnected events, has been achieved. From the fall of the first civilizations to the rising of the last, the story is told as one chronological study. An Anthropological approach, facilitates the tracing of connections between culture, the rise of political ideologies, and subtleties within languages and artistic expression, to enhance the understanding of these historical events.

We are now in the midst of a new inevitable awakening. But we must first understand the ideological war being waged and which side we are on. This war has its roots over hundreds of years of history, between the Latins and the Aryans. The Latin identity is simply anyone with even a drop of Black blood and is traced from the movement of Africans throughout the world; but while the Aryan is a pure-blooded Caucasian (an imaginary concept), the Caucasian is not necessarily Aryan. The distinction is like our modern-day Jihadists as a distinct group of Muslims, that do not represent all Muslims. Aryans, Saxons, Vandals and Scythians are the various historic terms, used to identify the "White" rebels who have the infamous legacy of destruction, very much like Jihadists. Their agenda is to subjugate the world under the ideology of White supremacy.

A Summary of this Book

We think of revolutions as some elaborate turnover of governments, but a revolution takes place when a group of people, begin to think differently about something and this change in perception turns the world around. This new world view, is the revolutionary current which propels the change in direction and triggers all the events which we associate with revolutions. [4]"For the last one hundred and forty-five years the fire of revolution has smoldered steadily beneath the ancient structure of civilization, threatening to destroy to its very foundations, that social edifice which eighteen centuries had been spent

Figure 1 Images of Mary and Jesus throughout Europe now called Black Madonnas

in constructing." This massive revolutionary current, changed the world from Black to White. In the twinkle of an eye, everything was changed. As a result, a dramatically new white centered story replaced millenniums of history.

This new story, dates back to the presidency of Thomas Jefferson in 1801. He is the dividing line between the Old-World Order and the new. Before Jefferson, most of the leaders on the global stage, including the Romans and many of the monarchs of Europe, were not considered White. God was imagined as Black and Cathedrals around the world including Europe had stained glass images and statues of Mary and Jesus now called *Black Madonna's*. This is going to take a little time to sink in, but the lens with which you now observe the world, is a relatively new one. It is only about two centuries of thousands of years of Earth history. Most of the materials from, before, shortly after and even during this period reveal this gradual transition.

By tracing the transfer of wealth, theology, culture and language, the trajectory of development becomes apparent. In every society since the beginning of civilization, the wealthy have always represented a tiny fraction of the population. Today less than five percent of Americans control, or have greater access to more than ninety percent of the wealth. Factoring this statistical imbalance, will also help to recast the contributions of Blacks at the foundation of society. This elevates the contributions of Black Americans to be of greater value and more significant to the shaping of American culture and identity than previously recognized. Their contributions speak volumes of the positions that they must have occupied in the stratification of American society; because slaves by definition, would have had little resources. Thus following the trail of money, will lead to a reconsideration of who was responsible for the development of nations, through the first Banks, Schools, hospitals, churches and factories. Necessity being the mother of invention, their exposure and intimate connection to the development of the country is made evident through their inventions.

In the beginning, gold was the standard currency, and Fort Knox was literally the fabled Timbuctoo, which had been guarded for centuries. The Black immigrants held the power and money

---

[4] Webster, Nesta World Revolution The Plot Against Civilization, Small, Maynard & Co Publishers Boston pg. viii

which they started to import into Europe during the reign of Mansa Musa around the fourteenth century, (the Dark Ages). But by [5]"the eighteenth century, the population of most European nations grew rapidly... and many parts of continental Europe still failed to produce enough to feed their own population." So the overwhelming White population from the Caucasus began to descend, into the established regions. It was once taught, that White Europeans went to Africa to capture Black laborer's, but an indepth investigation would question why Africa, when England and Ireland were so grossly overpopulated that men from Jonathan Swift in the seventeenth century to Thomas Malthus in the nineteenth, were proposing the most inhumane means to exterminate them. Antiquated weapons could not restrain the large and constant incursions of people from the North, so the aristocratic class fled Europe, to settle in the New World. They could have carried people from this vastly overpopulated region with them but travelled to Africa.

But the Aryans followed their tracks and raided their new settlements where ever they fled. By 1801 the Aryans had control of Spain, England, France and America, and Jefferson devised a plan that would allow them to take control of the whole world. They set their sights on complete world domination. This involved, not only the invasion and usurpation of territory, but the assumption of the history of the territories with the transplantation of millions of Caucasians through "colonization." They took on the identity of those they conquered. This was the [6]Gilded age and during this time, "European" History was intentionally and actively covered up with a golden veneer and supplemented with *alternative facts*. From the beginning of Jefferson's presidency, an organized and covert association began to lay the foundation for this New World Order. One which literally turned the world upside down. Those at the top were pushed to the bottom and the bottom became the top, so slaves became Massas and the Massas were enslaved. Many roles were reversed, so that traitors like Jefferson became heroes, and roles of prominence were altered, like the beloved Benjamin Franklin, who may have been Benjamin Banneker.

But just as Rome was not built in a day, these pioneers knew that this new story required generations of masons who would build this *invisible empire*. Jefferson first needed to get the members of the American government out of his way and he achieved this, not through diplomacy, but as [7]"a hypochondriac, he wrote the last chapter of history with his pistol." By the end of Jefferson's presidency, roughly forty-eight of the fifty-six men who signed the declaration of independence and comprised the infant government were dead. It was now essentially a new government. Laws were then enacted to diminish, and THEN enslave the Black population. Black communities like Seneca Village New York (now Central Park) were systematically dismantled and infiltrated to reduce their representation, and the estates of the most prominent and powerful

Figure 2. 1937 Kentucky flood by Margaret Bourke White

---

[5] The World an Illustrated History edited by Geoffrey Parker Harper row publishers New York 1986 338

[6] Term used by Mark Twain to describe the 19th century phenomenon of polishing and concealing information.

[7] Mapp, Alf J. A Strange Case of Mistaken Identity: Madison Books NY, London 1987 pg134 253 & 346

4

founding Americans, the Morris' were confiscated.

After 1801 new laws were passed to ban the immigration of Blacks. Ships which arrived at American ports carrying Blacks were labelled as illegal slave ships. While the flood gates were opened to transfer boat loads of "poor, tired and weak," White immigrants. They were given land, citizenship and the right to vote to affect the political makeup of the government; and arrived to find an abundance of open fields filled with food, and acquired the territory that those who planted the foundations of this nation, were denied. As these new immigrants climbed their way out of the American slums and into suburbia, they left behind the Blacks who remained the perpetual object of scorn and oppression. Blacks were selectively lynched or pushed off of their properties, and in some cases their children were kept as slaves. New laws were then passed to deny them the right to vote, bring a complaint to court or even read. Before long the allure of this American dream captivated many of the immigrants to assimilate into the illusion of a master race. Benjamin Franklin correctly predicted, that [8]"the invading Saxons would engross as many offices and exact as many tributes on the labor of the conquered to maintain their new offices. Then they would discourage their marriages to diminish them, while the Saxons increased on their abandoned lands." By the second and third decades of the nineteenth century, a heavier flow of German immigration set in. [9]"The vast increase in the number of immigrants-nearly a million arrived each year…" simply diluted the concentration of Blacks. Since then the fight for honorable inclusion in the general story has been futile. Historians prefer to perpetuate racial tension and division, by depicting Blacks as the bystanders or benign extras of the story.

Thus in an effort to combat the rising tide of bigotry about them, Blacks started to keep their own records and tell their own stories; but this effort actually aided the usurpers in cementing their version. Black history simply became a segregated tale of otherness, a collection of facts disconnected from the established version, of the new White American story. The story that Black people were brought to the New World courtesy of White controlled and engineered slave ships, is an egotistical and narcistic story which flatters those who would prefer to be referred to as "masters" or "Conquerors." This is used to explain away every single citing of a Black person in art or literature. The description is what one would expect of a journalists' account of citing an Ape on the streets of New York. The explanation is generally the same, the Ape must have gotten loosed from a zoo. Just as the Ape would be considered out of place on the streets of Manhattan, Blacks have been successfully convinced that their role in world history was anomalous. They never left Africa unless chained or invited by one mentally superior.

During the civil rights movement of the 1960s, there was a desperate attempt to reverse this frame of reference, and a major emphasis was placed on a reinterpretation in world history. According to the National Council for the Social Studies, this reinterpretation was to include [10]"ethno-history, which is essential to tie the varied ethnic rivulets into the mainstream of human history." This is because of the extent to which **historical scholarship was engaged in rewriting history** and as a result, "the gap widens between dependable knowledge and what is taught." The council believed that the eventual production of balanced world histories would contribute to political stability; but warned that if impartial scholars do not reconstruct these histories scientifically, then "partisans will fabricate faulty histories or create modern myths." And today modern myths abound, because this movement was subtly but actively resisted by academic establishments. Thus, modern histography, continues to relate the events of the past

---

[8] The founding Fathers, Benjamin Franklin in His Own Words. Thomas Fleming Newsweek NY 1972p102

[9] Spiller, Robert etal Literary History of the United States, 3rd ED 1963 pg. 679.

[10] Engle, Shirley New Perspectives in World History. 34th year book of the National Council for the Social Studies. 1964 (583-583). (582-583) & (Foreword VII)

5

as a series of disconnected facts, instead of a continuous process of transition and transplantation. Race and ethnicity are left to be implied, but generally subtle hints from erroneous pictorial representations are provided, so that general misconceptions become ingrained over time.

While a complete ethnographic reconstruction of all the individuals involved is impossible, (mostly because many of the early records were burned) what is certain, is that, a substantial number of the Blacks who immigrated to early North America, were key the figures in the developing society and on the world stage. They remove the gild of the new story, where the default American was White, and highlight how Black Americans played a dominant role in laying the foundation of American society. Once the tiny number of tycoons and aristocrats were killed off, they were robbed of their identities, their property, their children and slaves. Then every Black narrative, was simply chained to the legacy of slavery. The Black man became the figurative Ape; so that his presence away from his jungle home always begs an explanation. Many images were deliberately designed to convey this idea. The images reflect the artistic license and angle of the artist without regard for historical accuracy. By demanding authentic reproductions in lieu of artist renditions, this generation will reject the artificial lens of White supremacists and step out of this great farce. To claim victory against racial inequality and discrimination in the twenty first century, there must be a concerted effort to reopen the investigation of the stories that we have been told. This will shatter the lens which we have used to observe the world and ourselves, because the one who controls the lens will ultimately control much more than the past and present. The one who controls this lens, will control the future.

Figure 3 by Isaac Cruikshank This image is not only a false generalization, but it also represents the aim of psychological conditioning which has successfully reduced Black people to caricatures for the amusement of White Supremacist. It will be difficult to wrest this image from the mind, but facts have a way of dispelling myths.

Assignment

This book represents an organic, scientific reconstruction, which was generated through inquiry and in the various sections of the book, students or researchers are asked to think about their own questions, or interpretations, or what more could be added. Also, try to identify the following strategies which have been employed to keep control of the story.

Fire: Whenever a researcher arrives at information which seems inconsistent, conducting a firsthand investigation becomes impossible, because the original would have been burned or altered in some way.

Fillers: vague, obscured, and meaningless details added between two periods, so that it is difficult to connect a preceding period from a succeeding one.

Chronological disorder: one of the greatest techniques to reduce any intellectual connections between facts, is the simple change in order so that what would have been a catalytic event, is recorded as a simple rearrangement of insignificant facts.

Omission or alteration: simply leaving out pertinent details which would help to paint a more accurate picture, or deliberately erasing terms related to information which has been destroyed or altered. Some examples include, the complete ejection of the term Creole, or the redefinition of words like "Ottoman" to represent a foot stool or Moor to represent "dirt."

First: Just as a mother documents the milestones in her child's progress, like the first step, the simple designation of "first," reinforces the image of a group of newly developing people. It confines Blacks into the perimeter outlined by this artificial timeline. The Black researcher would not look past a certain point because we are told that the story begins here. Quite often, while the label is correct, its interpretation is intended to be misleading. Most African American firsts are American firsts.

Juxtaposition: the placement of images or other information, which lead the reader to imply something that the writer knows to be false but cannot explicitly state. As in the example below:

Figure 4 Ape Observatory in the Bronx Zoo. African children on the left, positioned near the Apes prominently featured center of the image. Caption for the African children reads, "The next generation..." While the Ape colony is featured with a new baby.

Misappropriation: Ascribing credit to others, or simply mislabeling it. Like generalizing the Arabian identity as White skinned, and then ascribing this identity to Moorish history.

Focus: A neurotic concentration on one aspect of the story, so that it is possible to completely change the story altogether. This last strategy focuses so intently on the condition of Black slaves, that slavery appears from inception, to apply exclusively to Blacks. This is achieved by using syllogistic tools, which would lead the reader to infer if this, then that.

- Most slaves in America were Black
- Many Whites believed that Blacks were inferior
- Therefore, whites were the Masters and Blacks were their slaves.

Who is the Niger

Figure 5 Depiction of early converts of Mohammed seeking sanctuary in Ethiopia at the court of the Christian emperor, The Negus, from the World History compiled in 1300 in Iran.

In the early twentieth century, the [11]Niger was classified, [12]"Improperly or loosely as a member of any dark-skinned race as an Indian, Filipino or an Egyptian... and at that time usually contemptuous." While the word was used with contempt by Whites, it was a term of endearment and respect for Blacks.

[13]*"Neger, which seems to have been borrowed by the early colonists from some Northern dialect of English, survived until the nineteenth century (*the gilded age*)." In* [14]*"1594 Amharic Negus or Kinged, King, was the title of the supreme ruler of Abyssinia (Ethiopia).* The Negus was first the commander of the army, a king among Kings. If the word is translated to mean General or Boss, then the difference in its application begins to make sense. "What up Boss," meant a different thing depending on who said it. While Blacks used the term as a salute of mutual respect and celebration, Whites used the word to mock them, after they had subdued and defeated them. This contempt, is the root cause of the lingering angry sentiments which the word continues to stir, and the terminology is an example of synoptic methods of oral retention. It illustrates how one word immortalizes a struggle and has the power to unite and divide and to conjure ancient wounds. But just as it is possible for a simple word to hold so much power, it is easily diffused by altering the word or its meaning, or by erasing it altogether. This was done when languages became standardized in the gilded era, in the mid-1800s. At that time, there were many variations of English even in England, where most educated people continued to use Latin. Thus, the English spoken in Ireland, differed from that spoken in England or America and varied even among Americans. Thus Neger, Naygar, Negus, Niga all mean the same thing, just as Amharic and Americ.

France was once the center of the globe and the French pronunciation for America is Americ, spelled differently but pronounced the same as the Ethiopian language Amharic. The people of France spoke French, England-English, Spain-Spanish and so the natives of America were probably considered Amharicans. Thus, the term Neger would have been derived from them. When Verrazano arrived in North America in the 16th century, he described the people he found on the east coast as:

---

[11] See end notes on other pronunciations.

[12] Webster, Noah. A Dictionary of the English Language: in Two Volumes, Volume 2, Black and Young, 1832

[13] ibid

[14] Oxford Universal dictionary reprinted with Addenda in 1955

Figure 6 a) Gouvernur Morris 1752-1818. The Morris Family lived in Bronx New York since the early 1600s B) 20th century African soldier

[15]of dark color like the Ethiopians, hair black and coarse, and not very long, which they tie together back on the head in the shape of a little tail. As for symmetry of the men, they are well proportioned, of medium stature, and rather exceed us. They have broad, arms well built, the legs and other parts of the body well put together…they incline to broadness of the face… Verrazano indicates that the native Americans were predominantly Negro. The Neger must have been the early colonists' reference to the Ethiopian Negus, it is an indication that the Niger's/Negus came in search of new turf to build their individual kingdoms, each with the prospect of becoming a boss in his own right.

The term 'Niger' has been used to generalize, define, degenerate, confine and diminish the understanding of the particular African identities in the Western World. Before the early twentieth century, Blacks were distinguished as Creoles, Jews, Moors, Arabs, Gypsies, Tartars and a great variety of distinctions between various groups of Blacks. Many lived throughout Europe, including Amsterdam the Netherlands, Bohemia, Austria and even Russia. While the term Niger appears to have been a title of great honor, it is not necessarily synonymous with Negro. The term Negro was also used among Spanish speakers in the Americas, with the same affection. This explains the persistence of the term; and its wide spread application from the wooly haired Negro, because of interracial and cultural integration, which has given birth to a multi ethnic appellation, which includes [16]White Negro's.

The fact is, people moved all around the world and paired with others to create the varied racial and language dynamics evident today. The popular national classifications we assume today only emerged during the French revolution around the late 1780s. Before this era European nationality, like an American nationality, did not convey homogenous ethnicity. The term European is largely of contemporary origin. Before the revolution, French, Russian or English did not automatically correspond to a Caucasian; but Goths, Visigoths, Vandals, Scythians, Saxons, Aryans and Gauls did. In many cases, German or Saxon is analogous to Caucasian to describe the physical characteristics of the people. But the concept of a national identity, was only created through the relatively recent extermination of millions of *Blacks* from Europe. Then reinforced by the artificial borders, which later restricted their immigration.

This book is centered around three of the most popular and distinct groups of Black Europeans, which are, the Moors, Jews and Creoles. It traces their history from Africa to Europe and then uncovers their movement to the west, to flee from the genocides of World War I and II less than a century ago.

---

[15] The New Larned History for Ready Reference, Reading and Research: The Actual Words of the World's Best Historians, Volume 1 Josephus Nelson Larned 1524- Page 273 Verrazano's voyage along the Atlantic coast of North America. This Italian navigator was the first *European* to sight New York and Narragansett bays.
(The Chinese are believed to have made it to the New World, as early as the 11th century.
*In the various editions of the Norvus Orbis, which detail Amerigo Vespucci's four voyages, Ramusio has given an abridgement in Italian of the third and fourth voyages only (his attention being chiefly directed to the results of Southern and African explorations). *The First Four Voyages of Amerigo Vespucci By Amerigo Vespucci
[16] Spiller, Robert etal Literary History of the United States, 3rd ED 1963 pg. 1412 "The Plight of the "White Negro," described vividly by Mailer." The process of creating an "Americanized," identity. A fusion between Black and White, Paul Robeson's book, "White Nigers," also captured this essence of whites in Russia.

The Moors

The Moors were the original inhabitants of all of North Africa, which was once part of the ancient Phoenician, Carthagian and then Roman Empires, defined as [17]"natives of the northern coast of Africa, called by the Romans from the color of the people, Mauritania, the country of dark complexioned people. The same country is now called Morocco, Tunis, Algiers, &c." (moor, mohr, maure; dark or obscure). Mauritania once covered most of North Africa, and today it is only a tiny fraction of its original size. According to the Oxford Universal dictionary reprinted with Addenda in 1955 "the Moors were supposed to be mostly Black or very swarthy and hence the word has often been used for 'Negro'."

Moor, Maur, Maure Mor, Moro, Morris, Moorish and many other variations, signify a relationship with or derived from the Moors. Following the path of money and knowledge helps to illustrate the trajectory of development. The Moors were the very wealthy and established Black minority who laid the foundation of European civilization. In the thirteenth century and especially during the reign of Mansa Musa around the fourteenth century, (the Dark Ages), these North and East Africans, were aggressively moving away from the encroaching Sahara region, to settle in more hospitable territory. Thus, the Black immigrants came with the money and experience, which they started to import throughout the world especially Europe.

Figure 7 Ludwig Deutsch (1855-1935) paintings est approx. 1million dollars at Sotheby's. Moors Guard Austrian Palaces.

Jews/Hebrews or Israelites

One of the last Biblical records of Jewish migrations, is a reference of the prophet Jeremiah and his group, traveling into Egypt in the 6th century BC. Then by [18]"250 BC a Greek Translation of the Hebrew Bible, called the Septuagint, is compiled by Jewish scholars living in Alexandria Egypt." From this point, their patterns of migration appear to coincide with the development of different regions from Greece, Rome France and by the 15th century, there is a concentration of Jews in Spain and Portugal. The Jews today are

---

[17] Webster, Noah. A Dictionary of the English Language: in Two Volumes, Volume 2, Black and Young, 1832
[18] National Geographic Explorer December 2011pg 121

identified as Caucasians, but this is a contemporary description. In the 18th century, the [19] Jews especially those still living in Portugal and Spain were considered to be, typically Black with the exception of a few in Germany.

That is the Myftery. Tis also a vulgar Error that the *Jews* are all black; for this is only true of the *Portuguese Jews,* who marrying always among one another , beget Children like themselves, and consequently the Swarthiness of their Complexion is entail'd upon their whole Race, even in the Northern Regions. But the *Jews* who are originally of *Germany ;* those , for Example, I have seen at *Prague,* are not blacker than the rest of their Countrymen.

Figure 8 A comparison between a) American Frederick Douglas b) German Jew Karl Marx c) German Jew Albert Einstein d) Black Russian Aleksandr Sergeyevich Pushkin

[20]"Many of the Jews who fled Spain and Portugal in the 16th century settled in Holland and England… and in the 17th century at Recife in Eastern Brazil, Curacao, Surinam, Guyana, Barbados and Jamaica." Other's returned to Africa, and in the 16th Century Leo Africanus noted that the King of Mali so hated the Jews in Africa, that he maliciously captured and sent many into slavery.

Creoles

In the beginning of American history, the vast majority of people in the Americas were considered [21]"Creoles." Because historically, Blacks created a distinction between the descendants of those who immigrated from Europe, (mostly France) called Creoles, and those who immigrated from Africa, called Negroes. This was applied [22]"originally to a person born or naturalized in the West Indies and other parts of America, Mauritius etc: country but of European negro race… as distinct from one freshly *imported* from Africa." Many were Black nobles and aristocrats exiled from Europe, who sort out Africans to fill their new colonies, and defend it against the new ruling commoners of Europe. Today

---

[19] A new voyage to Italy: with curious observations on several other countries, as: Germany, Switzerland, Savoy, Geneva, Flanders, and Holland; together with useful instructions for those who shall travel thither, Volume 1, Part 1 Maximilien Misson Printed for R. Bonwicke, 1714 pg. 139

[20] The Bible Through the ages. Reader's Digest Association Pleasanville NY Montreal 1996 pg 342

[21] A Philosophical and Political History of the British Settlements and trade in North America: by Abbe Raynal in two volumes. Vol II. EDINBURGH: pg. 162-163

[22] Oxford Universal dictionary reprinted with Addenda in 1955 pg 421

11

Creoles are identified as people from Louisiana, Haiti, Dominica, Guadeloupe, my island St. Lucia, and other areas which retain a form of "Creole" language or culture.

Saint Lucian Creole is spoken off the coast of East Africa, in Seychelles, Reunion and Mauritius and at the end of the 19th century, [23]many of the creoles of Mauritius and Reunion were of Zanzibar origin, and the creole language, though French in its vocabulary, is Bantu in its grammar. According to Steere "You may hear in the Creole of Mauritius the folk-lore that you have heard in the Swahili of Zanzibar. When he went to Mauritius he "was surprised to find the great similarity between creole folklore and that of Zanzibar." [24]Zanzibar became a port colony in 1503 and in the early 20th century, Rudyard Kipling witnessed that men were sent there to be trained into Admirals." If the Creoles, originated from Zanzibar, which was a port colony and military base, then it is evident that many were wealthy merchants or soldiers, who traversed the globe long before the arrival of Europeans. That their language appears to form some connection with French is indicative of the length of a shared culture and interaction. I visited Zanzibar in 2015, to conduct a survey of the various languages, and was surprised by the similarities, between this island and St. Lucia. As soldiers, their presence can be discovered in the relics of war in Louisiana, and the creole islands. These areas retain this legacy in their culture.

Saint Lucians have reenacted their European history of the war of the roses, for the past two hundred years, and among the very earliest settlements of a few thousand people, there were already hundreds of last names. This in a small island with a population of ninety percent Blacks. The fact is, many of these people are descendants of the nobility which was over thrown and exiled from Europe.

Figure 9 1" Women from Guadeloupe, display West Indian garb at Ellis Island in 1911." dignified and seemingly unimpressed, dressed in the "wob dwiyet," attire still considered an artifact of creole heritage by Caribbean Creoles especially Saint Lucians

Many of the last names represent the exiled nobility of France, England Prussia and other parts of Europe. Like George, Charles, and the friends of Louis king of France, "Jean Louis" or soldiers like Casimir from Poland and Lafayette from France, and a long list of generals who defeated both the new English and French commoners in many battles, to secure these islands. Some appear to be Moorish names like Morris or Mariuce. The Indian is also very similar to the mixture of people on the East Coast of Africa in countries like Madacasgar; with names like MalayKhan (mixed with the Khans) malay is a creole term which means to mix. Mixed with Asians or mixed with Khans. The picture on the left was taken in 1911, at the same time that Jack London witnessed the White citizens of London England, in such depravity that he referred to them as "the people of the Abyss." These migrants from the lowest depths of Brutish society, arrived

[23]Steere, Edward, and A. C. Madan. A Handbook of the Swahili Language, as Spoken at Zanzibar. 3d ed. London: Society for Promoting Christian Knowledge, 1884. Print. (6, 348,

[24]Kipling, Rudyard: Letters of Travel, Garden City New York. Doubleday, Page & Co. 1920

to instantly take their place above the caste which had been created for the Blacks. Caribbean immigrants were so amazed at the condition of Black Americans, that this reinforced the need to preserve their traditions. Today a new history, states that the traditional creole attire, the Madras or Wob Dwiyet, worn in creole countries like St. Lucia, were copied by slaves from their French masters. These erroneous attempts at cultural appropriation, simply play to the perception, that all Black civilizations copied their manners from a superior European.

The "nation," which were the Saxons who invaded France entered *sans cullotes,* literally *without pants.* Thus, creole attire was not modeled after those who invaded the kingdom, but came with those who fled to these countries. Unlike the vast coasts of the American Continent, the islands were more easily defendable, so that in the case of St. Lucia, the émigrés were able to keep hold of the island after fourteen wars against the new rulers of Britain and France, hence the cultural preservation.

Figure 10 The Intervention of a Shabine woman. Revolt in Bastille Prison Paris 1789 By Jacques Louis David 1799

The American Niger

The character traits of the American Niger, finds unbelievable parallels to the historical and contemporaneous story of the Massai, one of the most fascinating groups of any people I've ever encountered. The Massai, are legendary soldiers, whose world renowned militaristic, cultural identity can be traced as far back as the Egyptian empire. These soldiers were commissioned around the world to defend many empires, so their historic role provides a continuity between eras. Their language has great affinity to Latin, which may be the root of the languages which later evolved from a merger with them. Their military and musical choreography, inspired the rudiments of many musical instruments. Like the ram's horn, which has evolved into modern day brass instruments, like the trumpet or saxophone.

The American Niger, militant in almost every cultural expression, including dress, language, music and art, is believed to be their offspring. As the central figures of the story, they also provide the background music which denotes a change of scenery. So that the American culture and story has progressed through time by the changing rhythms echoed from the soul of these people. From the pits of slavery, chronicled by the Blues, to the emergence from this pit, to rhythm and Blues, and then the smooth sounds of their renaissance captured through Jazz as it later evolved into the progressively aggressive sounds of Bebop, Hip-hop and Rap. Because of this militant nature, every experience can find some connection to a battle, like a rap or dance battle. A tradition which persists among Afro-Brazilians,

13

through a martial arts dance technique called Capoeira. It is also imbedded in the culture of gangs, from the tradition of soldiers who were trained to remain idle and available for battle. Their secret hand gestures and code language, were reconstituted to render a complete distinction from any other group in the Americas. Once the contemporaneous writings are analyzed against the background rhythm, it opens a three-dimensional image of the past, filled with sound and emotion.

Keeping this militant characteristic, and history of Africa in the background, will revolutionize the process of reconstruction. If every step is molded by this type of inquisition and interrogation, the researcher must now analyze the following questions:

Is it possible, that in the age of navigation, that two whole continents were named after one man, Amerigo Vespucci, of whom little is known, or is it more plausible, that the continent was filled with Americ people? That these people were also the original Latin people and that their prevalence and persistence led to the appellation Latin Amhericans.

"Why would "White Europeans" invite such a militant people to inhabit their new territory, especially at a time when the population in Europe was exploding to unsustainable levels? Why would navigators leave New England and journey to Africa not England to find Africans?

Then, how could they have subdued these fierce experienced warriors, in an age of hand to hand combat, without the technology of mass produced revolvers? Now consider the analogy of a densely-populated nation like China. Why would Chinese speculators, trying to lay claim to the islands in the Pacific, go to India to capture Indian slaves to live in their new territory, which they were busy defending against a sea of contenders, including other Indians. This means that there are a few holes in this story.

The task of the Aryan, has been to diminish the value of the African, by portraying an image of a menial, dispensable puppet, held hostage to the strings of the master minded puppeteer. This story relies on a root, tens of thousands of years into the past, but with thousands of years of disconnected history. This massive gap in time, is filled with the cunning aid of scientific theories. The researcher imagines man's evolution from the African Abyss, where a series of climatological adaptations leads him to take "A great leap forward." This leap, simply skips over the transitional stages of history, and avoids the chronological steps by which the Aryan attains supremacy over the world. After arriving in Europe 30,000 years ago, the researcher following the trail of the Aryan, is left out in the cold, forced to shelter in caves and dugouts, surviving on raw meat and shrubs for *thousands* of years, well into the dark ages in the fourteenth century. Until finally, the evolved Aryan, discovers that the world is round and begins to lead the ignorant African to discover his "New World," even though he finds him already there. To overcome this inconvenient fact, all Blacks in the New World have been relegated to the same story of slavery and subjugation. Every citing is as anomalous as finding a wild animal, out of place in civilization. Thus, the mastery of this tale, is the literal scattering and disassociation of facts. Once all of the facts are arranged together, the anomaly disappears, and the folly is uncovered.

It is hard to imagine, but England and Ireland as much of Europe were countries filled with depravity, not much different to 21st century Haiti, the poorest nation in the Western Hemisphere. There was no shortage of free labor, and if these laborers were the same people, who raised the massive structures throughout the continent, then they would have been competent enough to lay the foundation of America; so why were Africans selected to lay the foundation of America.

A Contrast between Europe and Africa from the 16th to 18th Century

The state of England and Ireland from the seventeenth to the beginning of the twentieth century is worth noting. Every argument which rationalizes the invitation of Africans, in preference to Europeans creates a backdrop of a wealthy and powerful nation filled with aristocrats. These wealthy Englishmen, we imagine, sitting poised with their pinkies erect and sipping tea. We have been told that they were not accustomed to the hard labor and tillage, which laid ahead in laying the foundation for American society. But at this time [25]"In England, the cities were rife with degradation engendered by poverty, crowding, diseases and idleness, while in Ireland as in most of Europe, the peasantry was hounded to harvest more than the soil could produce." In the 1700s Jonathan Swift (1667-1745) described Ireland as a country completely neglected by government; with too many children to feed and a rise in prostitution which perpetuated the cycle. Swift's proposal to remedy the problem was to "eat the children." Seriously, Swift said: [26]"Infant's flesh will be in season throughout the year. I believe that no gentleman would repine to give ten shillings for the carcass of a good fat child... the mother would reap a profit and be fit for work till she produces another child."

In-fact whereas the population of the entire Globe represented only 500 million people in 1650, (less than half the population concentrated only in China today) [27]"in the eighteenth century, the population of most European nations grew rapidly... and many parts of continental Europe still failed to produce enough to feed their entire population." [28]Thomas Malthus' (1766 –1834) solution to the unsustainable rise in the European population, was to let people starve and to punish them for having

(2) "Mr. Malthus tells us, that the way to reduce our poor-rates is to persuade the lower orders to continence; to discourage them, as much as possible, from marrying; to preach wedding-sermons to them, if they will marry, upon the immorality of breeding.—that being a luxury reserved only for those who can afford it; and if they will persist in so improper and immoral a practice, after so solemn and well-timed a warning. to leave them to the punishment of severe want, and rigidly deny all parish assistance. No public relief is to be given to the starving infant; it is worth nothing to society, for its place will be presently supplied. and society, therefore, has no further business than to hang the mother, if she should shorten the sufferings of her babe rather than see it die of want. The rich are to be called upon for no sacrifices; nothing more is required of them than that they should harden their hearts. That we may not be suspected of exaggerating the detestable hard-heartedness of his system, we present it in his own language." *Southey.*
—I. E.

children. Malthus proposed to engineer famines, through a reduction of imported food. He believed that

---

[25] Calkins Carroll. Etal, The Story of America, Readers Ass. Inc Pleasantville NY Digest 1975 p. 9

[26] Swift Jonathan, A modest proposal for preventing the children of Ireland from Being a Burden on their Parents and Country. Man and Society 7. 45

[27] The World an Illustrated History edited by Geoffrey Parker Harper row publishers New York 1986 338

[28] The works of Lord Byron Canton XII Don Juan (2) Malthus

nature produced famine and plagues to keep this problem of population growth in check. [29]We must resign ourselves to periodical reductions of overpopulation by famine, pestilence, or war.

Low wages were justified to keep poor people from having the incentive of reproduction. Those who did find employment were subjected to hardship and [30]"instances of steady systematic cruelty, in the treatment of their children, which went far beyond anything recorded of slave drivers in (America). In the factories of Great Britain there were helpless children not only kicked and beaten but liable at any moment to receive a mortal wound from the Billy-roller of an exasperated slubber." Yet, it is at this time that historians tell us that Eli Whitney's cotton gin sparked a demand for slaves, and this demand led to the importation of slaves miles and months away in Africa. But Whitney's invention should have reduced the demand for slaves not increase it. [31]"Whitney calculated that a hand machine could do the work of ten slaves, and fifty if it was driven by water." The invention was mass produced without permission, instantly mechanizing what was once a laborious task. Thus, the demand for Africans could not have been linked to cotton. Especially since there was such a large number of unemployed people in England.

Even as late as 1901, England was [32]"still a place of immense disparities in well-being. While a few great landed aristocrats had virtually tax-free incomes of close to five thousand dollars a day, the working masses did well to earn five dollars a week." This relic of the Old-World system was observed by Jack London as late as 1902 when [33]"he plunged into London's East End, where humanity languished in one of its lowest depths. From his observations, he wrote "The People of the Abyss." "Year by year rural England pours in a flood of vigorous young life that perishes by the third generation... dying miserably at the bottom of the social pit called London." If European men were the captains of the sea, it would make sense that they would bring along their countrymen. This at the very least would save them from complete destitution. Instead these speculators travelled to Africa, why?

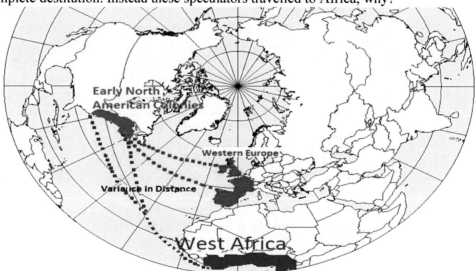

Figure 11 Map Adapted from the Northern Hemisphere by Sean Baker

---

[29] The Age of Napoleon: The Story of Civilization by Will Durant, Ariel Durant

[30]The white Slaves of England compiled from Official documents with twelve spirited illustrations by James Cobden, Miller, Orton & Mulligan, 1853 pg124

[31] Alistair Cooke's America, Alfred A knopf INc, New York 1973 Borzoi Books p193

[32] Britain Life World Library by John Oshborne NY 1961 Pg. 41

[33] University of Minnesota pamphlets on American writers no. 57 Jack London page 12 by Charles Walcutt 1966 North Central publishing co St. Paul

Because these wealthy philanthropists who laid the foundation of these societies, were themselves Africans. These wealthy aristocrats had long traversed the globe, and were the Romans, Moors of North Africa, Creoles of East Africa and Guineans of West Africa. When they arrived in Europe, from as early as the first century, as Roman soldiers, they immediately built fortresses and brought in their foreign armies and workers. Then [34]"in the fifteenth century, sizeable numbers of Blacks entered Europe. By the mid-sixteenth centuries, Blacks, slave and free constituted about ten percent of the Portuguese cities... Black servants were highly prized and sort after," because the nobility did not trust their Saxon subjects.

Before the French revolution, in the 18th century [35]John Knox' visited France, he described the women's customs of painting their skin white, which are naturally brown so "their faces are concealed under a false complexion. Their heads are covered with a vast load of false hair, which is frizzled so as exactly to resemble the wooly heads of the Guinea Negroes." [36] The diversity and distinctions of the earlier society are captured in the trend of covering the head with hair which resembled the "Negro's wool." This trend started around 1625 when full bottom wigs were introduced into Europe. This is also about the time when the Guinea company which was founded in 1588, received a charter from Charles I, and Guineans began immigrating into England. The system of government which they instituted, did not regard for the poor around them.

The concept of government and its branches of political responsibility for a nation, have a very different appearance today than historically. The top five percent were the government. They ruled the world and their scraps trickled down to the masses. This is the origin of trickle-down economics. Slavery was the universal system of employment, people who did not have the means to care for themselves, went into slavery. Before the concept of national boundaries, there was no obligation on the part of "government" to provide for their countrymen. In Europe anyone without means, Black or White was essentially enslaved, forced to become subjects to the aristocracy. Those who lived within their fortresses were called serfs, they were forced to remain within the domain of the nobles for security and survival; but the large population rendered forced servitude unnecessary on the part of the nobility. It is important to address the sharp contrast between the foreign nobility and their Saxon subjects; because many of the wars which would later erupt throughout European history, were turn overs of national or racial and political power.

The new diverse population began a process of integration which led to an amalgamation of languages now considered "Germanic;" but the fact is, the English or German language, did not receive an official form until the mid-19th century. The very first efforts to write in English and German, sheds light on the transitional stages and forms. Language is an area which has been greatly neglected, in the study of history. A shared language suggests a historic connection and level of familiarity or intimacy, which may be genetic or at the very least economical. The Gala island of Saint Helena in North Carolina, preserves the most ancient and extant artifact of the early Gallic dialect, which has a similar root to modern English and German. This language sounds very similar to English and the native "Pidgin" language of Senegal. It is part of the body of evidence which indicates that modern English takes its root from the Africans who migrated from the Guinean Empire.

---

[34]Mckay, John, Hill and Buckler, A History of Western Society from antiquity to the enlightenment. Sixth edition. Houghton Miffin Company 1999 Pg435-436

[35] A New Collection of Voyages, Discoveries and Travels: Containing Whatever is Worthy of Notice, in Europe, Asia, Africa and America, Volume 5 by John Knox J. Knox, 1767

[36] A Collection of Voyages and Travels, Volume 2 Awnsham Churchill Asian Educational Services, 1732 pg. 394

By stark contrast, Joannes Leo Africanus, 1494 - 1554 visited Some of the towns from the Mauritanian Empire, in the 16th century, and described [37]iron and gold industries, professors, physicians carpet weavers, shoe makers, and merchants from around the world coming to trade with the Africans. Alguechet was very wealthy nation West of Egypt, in the region of the Libyan desert filled with dates…The Citie of capes upon the Mediterreanean sea, "The inhabitants of the foresaide plaine are all Black people." "Of the Kingdom of Guber… here are also great store of artificers and linen weavers: and here are such shoes made as the ancient Romans were wont (known) to wear, the greatest part carried to Tombuto and Gago. Likewise here is abundance of rice, and of certain other grain and pulse, the like whereof I never saw in Italie. In this region there is a certain great village containing six thousand inhabitant families, being inhabited by all kinds of merchants. All the people he saw were Black and wealthy.

The image below was captured on my 2015 trip to Tanzania and its island city Zanzibar. These men are the Maasai of Tanzania. Their customs remained consistent among various parts of the country.

Figure 12 American in Orange shirt met Massai elders in June of 2015. The Massai wear a "Plade Bonet" fabric like the Black Scots and Irishmen in the 18ᵗʰ Century. This pattern is also noted in Harriet Beecher Stowe's story "Uncle Tom's Cabin. The elders remain at the home site with their hair shaved, while the young men which we met in the city, grow their hair long like their soldiers would.

In my brief interview with the Maasai, I discovered a great similarity between their language and Latin. These men may be related to the ancestors of those who immigrated to Rome, to help establish the Roman Empire. Their extensive radiation into the Americas led to the application "Latin" America, a term which is under extreme repression today. European scholars acknowledged this distinction between the so called Germanic Europeans and the Latins. Some claimed that the original Germans were [38]"less sensuous, passionate and vivacious, than the people of "Latin origin." [39]Winston Churchill described a

---

[37] The History and Description of Africa: And of the Notable Things Therein Contained by Leo (Africanus), Robert Brown, John Pory Hakluyt Society, 1896 pg. 776

[38] Outlines of German Literature by Joseph Gostwick & Robert Harrison Holt & Williams F. W. Christern 1873 p. 5

[39] Churchill, Winston A history of the English Speaking Peoples. The New World 18, Bantam Books INC New York 1956

contrast between the *Northern races* (of Aryan Germans) the *barbaric conquerors*, compared to the Latin races who were reaching a high development of practical politics. There was a clear distinction between the people in Southern and Western Europe from the Slavic peoples of North and Eastern Europe.

The interactions between Sanskrit, Swahili and Latin speakers and the idea that the very concept of money was connected to these navigators, led to the names of prominent trading stations in Germany like the 'Black Heads,' land Gutenberg, from the Southern African word for place of gold, 'Gauteng' and at least some of the people who sold and traded merchandise from all over the world, were possibly the Venda of South Africa, this has led to the name, Vendor the English word for merchant. As in Shakespeare's merchant (originally Moor) from Venice. These words are the oral artifacts of the earlier society.

Figure 13 Albrecht Dürer German painter, and mathematician Nuremberg. (1484–1490) Merchant bringing Pot of Gold

In the Old-World era money was weighed and literally traded as Guinean gold coins. The Africans controlled and monopolized the very system of wealth which was heavily guarded in their back yards. These mines and much of Africa were concealed from the outside world until relatively recently. There is one consistent pattern throughout history. It is that as the Latin people enter and begin to build, the, vandals invade to steal, kill and destroy. The latins influenced many civilizations from Egypt, Greece, and Rome, finally out of Europe entirely and now the Americas. Each time they were continuously forced to run from them. The story is that we would have to learn how to outrun the horses to stay alive. As a people we learned not only to run faster, but to endure to the end of the race and this is the end of the race. This contrast, between Africa and Europe is such an extreme departure from 21st century histography, that a brief discourse on World history is required to understand the complete transition from Black to White.

Restoring the Niger's place in World History.

They remain, the same yesterday, today as tomorrow, from Egypt to Asia, Greece, Europe, to America......

*14 **a**) Old Kingdom Pharaoh Khufu, Khêops or Cheops 4th dynasty 2580 B.C. (Egyptian Museum), Berlin by Einsamer Schütze **b**). Woman from the Lower Valley of the Omo River, Southern Ethiopia. UNESCO World Heritage Site, Source Vittorio Bianchi by Annamaria Donnoli **c**).Pharaonic hair dress. Egyptian Museum), Berlin by Einsamer Schütze **d**). Early 20th century Maasai man from Ethiopia*

This chapter simply establishes chronology and continuity, between the events leading to the birth of Aryan colonization; but more extensive coverage of various eras is provided in "Ourstory". It is important to go back to the root to fully comprehend how the story was ultimately changed. One feature very often identified with the general African diaspora, is a deep-rooted sense of spirituality; so deep that I found it impossible to tell the story without it. The whole study conjures up this spiritual sense.

Pasmetics, one of the last native Egyptian pharaohs (595-589 BC) represents the beginning of the fall of native Egypt around the 7th century BC. Before this period, Egypt was the longest enduring and most powerful civilization on Earth. The pharaohs were titled "sons of God" Genesis 6:2. From this region came forth the founders of sciences of medicine, military and political strategies, civil engineering and farming, mathematics, astronomy and the mastery of masonry among other things. The Ethiopians had a large army of renowned soldiers, and archers, mentioned in 2 Chronicles 14: 9. But from the reign of Pasmetics a state of continuous warfare prevailed; because in an effort to take control of the throne of Egypt against other possible heirs, [40] "he hired soldiers out of Arabia, Caria, and Ionia. Some of the kings of the other side were slain, and the rest fled into Africa, and were not able to further contend for the Kingdom. Then since he had gained the kingdom by the help of his foreign soldiers,

> Psammeticus entrusted them chiefly in the concerns of the government. The Egyptians were so incensed, that above two hundred thousand of them revolted, and marched away towards Ethiopia, there to settle themselves in new habitations. Psammeticus was kind and liberal to all strangers that came into Egypt... and was the first of all the kings of Egypt that encouraged foreigners to traffic in his country."

---

[40] The Historical Library of Diodorus the Sicilian: In Fifteen Books. To which are Added the Fragments of Diodorus, and Those Published by H. Valesius, I. Rhodomannus, & F. Ursinus, translated by G Booth ESQ Harvard College Library In two volumes. Vol. 1 by Diodorus (Siculus.) Chapter 5 pg. 69-71

The prophet Isaiah predicted that: five cities in Egypt would speak the language of Canaan and one of them would be called *the City of the Sun. (NIV) Isaiah 19:18

In the 1st century AD Pliny, a Roman politician, tried to explain how the Arabians got to Egypt because they were not Ethiopian or "dark skinned." According to Pliny, [41]"the people inhabiting along the sides of the Nile, from Syene to Meroe, are not Ethiopians, but Arabians, who for the sake of fresh water approached the Nile, and there dwelt: as also that *the City of the Sun, which we said before in the description of Egypt, standeth not far from Memphis, was founded by the Arabians." Some believed at the time that Arabia extended into the east coast of the Nile, but he believed they got there because they were looking for fresh water. The Egyptian language was also completely erased and replaced with the language of Canaan, Arabic. Eventually Egypt was completely overrun with Assyrians, who assimilated into the native population and so today speak Arabic the language of Arabia or Canaan. "My people went before time into Egypt to sojourn there; and the Assyrian oppressed them without cause." Isaiah 52:4

Ezekiel (622-570 BC) predicted that "Egypt would become the basest of Kingdoms; neither shall it exalt itself anymore above the nations." 29:15 that "their land will be sold to the wicked and *inhabited by strangers*" 30:12 and the pomp of her strength would cease: as for her, a cloud shall cover her, and *her children shall go into slavery.*"30:18. "And I will scatter the Egyptians among the nations, and disperse them throughout the countries." 30:23 Those who escaped into West Africa were eventually enslaved. Then "the Lord will stir up Egyptian against Egyptian—brother will fight against brother, neighbor against neighbor, city against city, kingdom against kingdom." Isaiah 19:2 The once impenetrable fortress of Egyptian brotherhood and nationalism, became divided and the state of battle a perpetual curse.

Egyptians and Nubian nobility began to disperse. They scattered throughout the world to regions like Greece, Phoenicia, Rome and as far as the Americas. The rise and fall of civilizations coincided with their entrance or exit. They brought with them their carefully guarded repository of ancient knowledge of masonry, sculpture, metallurgy, medicine, philosophy, astronomy, history, but also an unshakable pride.

Figure 15 a) Psammetrich_and God's wife statues Ägyptisches_Museum_Berlin by Marcus Cyron b)Pharos of the 25th dynasty c) probably represents Romulus and Remus the founders of Rome. The statues dated 6th century BC were discovered buried in Athens naked and Barefoot with hair overgrown. Isaiah 20:3 And the Lord said, like as my servant Isaiah hath walked naked and barefoot three years for a sign or indication and wonder upon Egypt and upon Ethiopia.1

Their first exodus coincides with the voyages of Hanno, the Bantu migrations into West Africa, the rise of Phoenicia and the transplantation of Egyptians throughout the known world including Persia and Greece.

---

[41] Pliny chapter 29 The Gulf of the Red Sea.

1. According to the Persians best informed in history, the Phœnicians began the quarrel. This people, who had formerly dwelt on the shores of the Erythræan Sea,² having migrated to the Mediterranean and settled in the parts which they now inhabit, began at once, they say, to adventure on long voyages, ₄₂ **freighting their vessels with the wares of Egypt and Assyria.³**

They migrated from Eritrea in East Africa, to settle throughout the world, and first surface under the Persian/Median empire as the immortal soldiers. Then in North Africa to establish Numidia, or New Media. Their migration pattern is also consistent with the voyages of Hanno, a Navigator of 500 BC, best known for the first documented exploration of the West African coast and its settlements. Hanno sailed to West Africa with sixty-five ships, and about thirty thousand people. Hanno founded cities, on the West coast of Africa and traveled as far South as Zimbabwe. Thus, establishing a trade route through the Sahara, which connected Ethiopians from the East to the entire continent. The rise of the flourishing Nok civilization in Nigeria, coincides with this expansion.

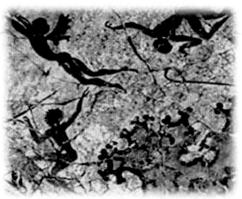

Figure 16. Date 3rd century BC shipwreck from Excavation at Akrotiri on the island of Santorini.

The East African development of writing systems evolved from Hieroglyphics to a symbol based Meroic script, then finally the Latin symbols from these Phoenicians of North Africa. ⁴³Letters came out of Phoenicia into Greece and the Egyptian priests, out of their sacred records bring arguments to prove that everything wherein the Grecians excel, and for which they are admired, was brought over from Egypt into Greece. These include their religious rites, fables and the exquisite art of the Stone-carvers in Greece, all of Egyptian extraction.

Phoenicians were the overseers of the sacred mysteries from Egypt, so that the priests were selected exclusively from members of their families. Thus, Grecian religious ceremonies and deities, evolved from Egyptian worship and essentially preserved the ancient culture of the Egyptians. These tall, dark and handsome figures were seen as Gods, and according to Diodorus the Sicilian, they returned annually to Ethiopia for a twelve-day feast at the Table of the Sun.

Figure 17 Sacrifice of Conon. Temple of the Palmyrene Gods in Dura-Europos. 1

---

⁴² History of Herodotus, Volume 1 page 121 Herodotus Halicarnasseus, George Rawlinson, Henry Creswicke Rawlinson (sir), John Gardner Wilkinson

⁴³ The Historical Library of Diodorus the Sicilian: In Fifteen Books. To which are Added the Fragments of Diodorus, and Those Published by H. Valesius, I. Rhodomannus, & F. Ursinus, translated by G Booth ESQ Harvard College Library In two volumes. Vol. 1 printed by W.M Dowall 1814 pg. 314-317

Figure 18a) Drawing found on cave walls in the Sahara dated to around 300BC B) Tembu women of South Africa display similar hair covering and clothing and white painted faces. By Margaret Bourke White

[44]Carlo Bergman discovered several way stations in the region of the Northern Chad Basin. These trade routes were also used between Egypt into West and South Africa. Among those who emigrated out of North Africa were probably the Tembu people who now inhabit South Africa. A caravan of women with similar facial markings and headress are depicted in the Sahara desert, dated around 300BC. According to Hanno, the Garamantes of the Niger region, used four-horse chariots, to chase the Ethiopians who could out run horses, and were swifter on foot than any nation in the world. These master charioteers were also recorded in Biblical narratives of Zerah the Ethiopian general, "with a host of a thousand, thousand, and three hundred chariots; and came unto Mareshah against them," (2 Chronicles 14:9 & 12) The prophet Jeremiah also recorded a message, which corresponds to Hanno's description of the Ethiopians he encountered in North Africa. "If thou hast run with the footmen, and they have wearied thee, then how canst thou contend with horses?" These runners were training to face an enemy so powerful that Jeremiah compared them to horses.

Figure 19 Tuareg Tribesmen from Niger a). by Marc Riboud/Magnum, As featured by the encyclopedia as a Southern Saharan Tuareg b). Modern Tuareg Clémence Delmas. The images depict a custom of head covering prevalent in early European art which evolved into the modern hoodie.

[45]In addition to being used in Phoenicia, the (Phoenician) language spread to many of its colonies. In one, the North African city of Carthage, a later stage of the language, known as Punic, became the language of the Carthaginian Empire. Punic was influenced throughout its history by the Amazigh language and continued to be used by North African peasants until the 6th century AD. Phoenician words are found in Classical Greek and Latin literature as well as in writings in the Egyptian, Akkadian, and

---

[44] Schneider, Thomas Journal of Ancient Egyptian Interconnections. University of Arizona online journal 2011

[45] http://www.britannica.com/EBchecked/topic/457164/Phoenician-languageTuareg accessed February 4th 2015

Hebrew languages. The language is written with a 22-character alphabet that does not indicate vowels. The Phoenician writing system survived in the tifinagh script of the Tuareg, who live in the southern Sahara. With their dispersal African [46]"modes of food production were spread to the far southern tip of the continent. The agents generally recognized in this process have been the Early Iron Age Bantu. These pastoralist ancestors of the present-day Bantu people, carried iron-working southwards, together with farming. Chariot engravings found in the desert show two wheeled chariots drawn by horses. The distribution of engravings suggests that these vehicles were used for trans-saharan trade."

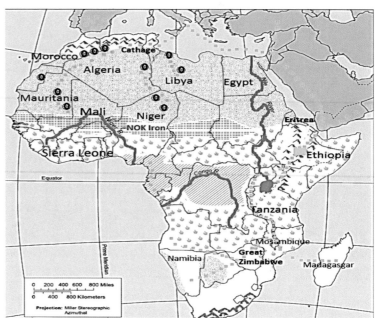

Figure 20 Map adapted from Arizona geographic Alliance to illustrate the chariot markers for routes of Bantu migration.

The dispersal of these people throughout the world can be traced through their influences in new regions. The Plantation systems found in the Americas were designed by these historic pastoralists. In the early twentieth century, Melville J. Herskovits visited West Africa to complete an anthropological assessment of the region. He discovered that one of the characteristics of all the villages which he visited, was the existence of an "expanse of tilled land consisting largely of farmers." His descriptions are reminiscent of the early American plantation systems.

Greece

Figure 21 Perseus 212-166 BC the last king of the Antigonid dynasty, in Greece

By around 300 BC Greece, gained prominence, but when Greece fell after many invasions by the Northern peoples, wealthy Grecians escaped to Rome. Rome then became the center of the world; but by the 5th century AD, a new group of Northerners, invaded Rome and a plague followed. It decimated the Romans, so that Rome fell also. Many fled back to North Africa. African theologian Augustine of Hippo or Saint Augustine (354– 430 AD), was the bishop of Algeria at the time, and a witness to the invasion and fall of Rome. His writings are considered to have laid the foundation of Western Philosophy.

[47]"By the first decade of the sixth century AD, the vandals were beginning to be absorbed into the mass of the Afro-Latin population. In this respect the religious and social history of North Africa resembles that of Burgundy, Spain and Italy." The spread of these Latin speakers from Rome, throughout Europe led to the creation of new languages called "Romance Languages."

---

[46] Past Worlds, the Times Atlas of Archeology edited by Chris Scarre. Pg202

[47] The Cambridge History of Africa, Volume 2 J. D. Fage, Roland Anthony Oliver, Cambridge University Press, 1978 pg. 483

The Romans

Figure 22 Fayum portraits discovered with the mummies of Romans in Egypt 2nd or 3rd century AD. Although some seem whitened, the features remain. Roughly six to eight hundred years after the fall of Egypt, two hundred years after the departure of Christ and numerous invasions. Notice that no one has straight hair.

Although many images have been whitewashed, the curly afros glossed over, they clearly depict Romans as having African ancestry. Note Pliny's opinion below about the differences between the most diverse people of Europe and those of Africa.

BOOK II.]   *History of Nature.*   117–119

CHAPTER LXXVIII.

The Reason of the Difference of Nations.

HEREUNTO we must annex such Things as are linked to celestial Causes. For it is beyond doubt that the Ethiopians, by Reason of the Sun's Vicinity, are scorched with the Heat thereof, like to them that be burnt, having their Beards and Hair curled. Also, that in the opposite Climate of the World to it, in the frozen Regions, the People have white Skins, Hair growing long, and straight, and yellow; but they be fierce by Reason of the rigorous Cold:

Egyptian and Cushite movement into the coastal regions of Africa and Europe are associated with a wave of Empires; but it is worth noting the condition of the people in Northern Europe who were beginning to descend at this time.

The Invaders
"Mask On"

[48]"All that can be said of the (Germanic races) with reasonable certainty is that at the time when Rome was beginning to assert herself in Southern Europe, these races were clustered around the shores of the Baltic and North Sea. The most westerly of the tribes had found no settled home when Julius Caesar came into conflict with them in the first century before Christ. These Germanic barbarians, for more than a century before his time had been a source of terror to the Roman world."

It is significant to establish the ethnic identities which are often omitted; because this allows the researcher to compare the identity of the invaders to the earlier population, it is then possible to see how the demographic change corresponds to a change in language, and that this is a recurring pattern. The following account is by Procopius, a sixth century eyewitness to the fall of the Roman Empire:[49]

> Now while Honorius was holding the imperial power in the West, barbarians took possession of his land; and I shall tell who they were and in what manner they did so. There were many Gothic nations in earlier times, just as also at the present, but the greatest and most important of all are the Goths, Vandals, Visigoths, and Gepaedes. In ancient times, however, they were named Sauromatae and Melanchlaeni;[1] and there were some too who called these nations Getic. All these, while they are distinguished from one another by their names, as has been said, do not differ in anything else at all. For they all have white bodies and fair hair, and are tall and handsome to look upon, and they use the same laws and practise a common religion. For they are all of the Arian faith, and have one language called Gothic; and, as it seems to me, they all came originally from one tribe, and were distinguished later by the names of those who led each group.

This singular Gothic language which all Northern people once spoke, may have been the original Slavic language. [50]"Low German, with which English, the language spoken in Holland, and Scandinavian languages are all closely connected," is one of *several variations* over the centuries. Tacitus a first century Roman politician, gave a similar account of the universal features of the Northern people, about four hundred years earlier, in his book Germanica. [51]"Tacitus no doubt, based his work upon authentic information. His description of these tall northern races with their fierce blue eyes and fair hair, brought the primitive simplicity of the Germans into contrast with the effeminate luxury of imperial Rome."

---

[48] A History of German Literature 6th Ed by J. G Robertson, William Blackwood & Sons LTD Edinburgh and London. 1949 p 14
[49] History of the Wars, Bks III and IV (Vandalic War) Translated by, Harvard University Press, 1916 pg9-11
[50] Outlines of German Literature by Joseph Gostwick & Robert Harrison Holt & Williams F. W. Christern 1873 p.1
[51] A History of German Literature 6th ED, by J. G Robertson, 1949 pg. 14-17

Source — C. Cornelius Tacitus, *De Origine, Situ, Moribus, ac Populis Germanorum* [known commonly as the "Germania"], Chaps. 4–24 *passim*. Adapted from translation by Alfred J. Church and William J. Brodribb (London, 1868), pp. 1–16. Text in numerous editions, as that of William F. Allen (Boston, 1882) and that of Henry Furneau (Oxford, 1894).

4. For my own part, I agree with those who think that the tribes of Germany are free from all trace of intermarriage with **Physical char-** foreign nations, and that they appear as a dis-**acteristics** tinct, unmixed race, like none but themselves. Hence it is that the same physical features are to be observed throughout so vast a population. All have fierce blue eyes, reddish hair, and huge bodies fit only for sudden exertion. They are not very able to endure labor that is exhausting. Heat and thirst they cannot withstand at all, though to cold and hunger their climate and soil have hardened them.

6. Iron is not plentiful among them, as may be inferred from ₅₂ the nature of their weapons.[1] Only a few make use of swords or

Note that the Romans considered that the Germans looked very different and distinct from them. Africa developed its own iron industry some 5,000 years ago, according to "a formidable new scientific work from UNESCO." [53]In Western Tanzania and adjacent parts of Rwanda, sophisticated brick-built furnaces were used on a large scale to produce what was technically a high carbon steel. It is clear that this industry was thriving by the last four centuries BC, and it may have been established significantly earlier. (These were the First Blacksmiths) These are the skills which they brought to Europe.

16. It is a well-known fact that the peoples of Germany have no cities, and that they do not even allow buildings to be erected close together.[4] They live scattered about, wherever a spring, or a meadow, or a wood has attracted them. Their villages are not arranged in the Roman fashion, with the buildings connected and joined together, but every person surrounds his dwelling with an open space, either as a precaution against the disasters **Lack of cities** of fire, or because they do not know how to build. **and towns** They make no use of stone or brick, but employ wood for all purposes. Their buildings are mere rude masses, without ornament or attractiveness, although occasionally they are stained in part with a kind of clay which is so clear and bright that it resembles painting, or a colored design. . . .

₅₄ **30** THE EARLY GERMANS

[52] The Source Book of Medieval History: Documents Illustrative of European Life and Institutions from the German invasion to the Renaissance by Frederic Austin 1908 pages 22-25 & 44-46

[53] Chris Scarre, Past Worlds The times atlas of Archaeology. Guild Publishing London 1988 pg. 202

[54] The source book of medieval history: documents illustrative of European life and institutions from the German invasion to the Renaissance by Frederic Austin 1907 pages 29-31

And now it will be worth while to declare that which multitudes are altogether ignorant of. Those who inhabit the inland parts beyond Massilia*, and about the Alps, and on this side the Pyrenean mountains, are called Celts; but those that inhabit below this part called Celtica, southward to the ocean and the mountain Hyrcinus, and all as far as Scythia, are called Gauls. But the Romans call all these people generally by one and the same name, Gauls.

For stature they are tall, but of a sweaty and pale complexion, red haired, not only naturally, but they endeavour all they can to make it redder by art. pg 314

The women here are both as tall and as courageous as the men. The children, for the most part, from their very birth are grey-headed; but when they grow up to men's estate, their hair changes in colour like to their parents. Those towards the north, and bordering upon Scythia, are so exceeding fierce and cruel, that (as report goes) they eat men, like the Britains that inhabit Iris†.

They are so noted for a fierce and warlike people, that some have thought them to be those that antiently overran all Asia, and were then called Cimerians, and who are now (through length of time) with a little alteration, called Cimbrians.

Antiently they gave themselves to rapine and spoil, wasting and destroying other countries, and slighted and despised all other people. These are they that took Rome, and robbed the temple at Delphos. These brought a great part of Europe and Asia under tribute, and possessed themselves of some of the countries of those they subdued. Because of their mixture with the Grecians, they were at last called Gallo-Grecians. They often routed and destroyed many great armies of the Romans. [55]

The entrance of these warlike Barbarians was associated with mass death, and destruction. There is a distinction between these Aryan jihadists and those who would become acculturated into the Latin world. This distinction is marked by dramatic changes to language, phenotypical features and religious customs, which eventually gave birth to a new people, and modern civilization. [56] "The prevalent overestimate of the Barbarians' contribution to Western society" can be traced to many false delusions... but Empires fell as a result of self-inflicted wounds. The Barbarians "were merely the vultures feeding on the carrion or the maggots crawling on the carcass." Toynbee, identified three factors which mark the transition from the old to new, but the most significant is "the displacement of the cradle of the new society from the original home of its predecessor... even though the frontier of the old society became, the center of the new one." This displacement credits the Barbarians with the development of society because they simply assumed the identity and history of those which they displaced and were then credited with the "development of certain institutions of self-government, which the Teutonic tribes were supposed to have brought with them from no-man's-land." This displacement conceals the truth because it takes the mind away from the question of origin.

How did these formerly Barbaric people become so powerful. Where is the source of the wealth which gave them the ability to travel the world? This is the reason for a brief survey of the Old World and an analysis of how the story changed from Black to White.

---

[55] The Historical Library of Diodorus the Sicilian: In Fifteen Books. To which are Added the Fragments of Diodorus, and Those Published by H. Valesius, I. Rhodomannus, & F. Ursinus, translated by G Booth ESQ
Harvard College Library In two volumes. Vol. 1 printed by W.M Dowall 1814 pg. 314-317

[56] A study of history by Arnold Toynbee. Abridgement of volumes I-VI Oxford University Press New York and London. 1946

African Dispersal throughout Europe 1-1658 A.D.
"Mask Off"

*Figure 23 **a)** Statue of Saint Maurice in Madeburg Germany. Wikimedia.orgUser Chris73-3.0 **b)** coat of arms of the Brotherhood of Blackheads displayed in Riga Russia and the Beriltz tour of Riga guide book 2016*

It has been taught that Christianity was first established as a political religion by Romans, under Constantine around 327AD; but Christianity was first embraced by the Ethiopians after the apostle Phillip baptized an Ethiopian priest, in the first century, Acts 8: 26-28. Ethiopia though overlooked by modern scholarship, played a pivotal role in the widespread establishment of the faith. Keeping in mind the military traditions of Africans, it is no wonder that these crusaders spread their faith to Egypt, North Africa and Rome, through the military. Then by the fourth century, when the Roman empire called for soldiers to beat back the constant invasion of Aryans, the Theban legion refused to harm the people because they professed the faith. [57]"St. Maurice, a third century patron saint of Magdeburg, Germany, was an Egyptian commander in the Roman army. His head adorned the coat of arms of the leading Nuremburg families, including Albert Durer, Germany's most famous Renaissance artist."

By the time of Constantine, the division between the pagan Roman government, and their Christian soldiers, forced Rome's hands. The Roman empire adopted Christianity as its state religion; but within a century Italy was invaded. The Romans succumbed to plagues brought in by the Northern people and in 476 AD the Roman Empire collapsed. Many returned to Africa, others moved to Western Europe to parts of Spain, France and the English Isles. [58]"By the first decade of the sixth century AD, the vandals were beginning to be absorbed into the mass of the Afro-Latin population. In this respect the religious and social history of North Africa resembles that of Burgundy, Spain and Italy." The spread of these Latin speakers, throughout Europe led to the creation of new languages called "Romance Languages."

[59]Then toward the end of the sixth century, when Britain, under the dominion of the Saxons was in a state of barbarianism and idolatry, Pope Gregory the great, struck with the beauty of some Anglo-Saxon youth exposed for sale in the market place at Rome, conceived a fancy for the race, and determined to send missionaries to preach the gospel among these benighted islanders. From then until the protestant

---

[57] Pearson, Heritage of World Civilizations

[58] The Cambridge History of Africa, Volume 2 J. D. Fage, Roland Anthony Oliver, Cambridge University Press, 1978 pg. 483

[59] The Works of Washington Irving volume 5 The New Hudson Edition P.F. Collier and son NY p527

Figure 24 Medieval Art depicting Black Monks Evangelizing Europe.

period, [60]the monastery in Stevenson Normandy had an alien priory of Black monks....and [61] the Justinian monastery held the Black Benedictine monks,

Then in 747 after [62]earthquake damage... many Arabians begun moving west. [63]"After the Mahumetans got the dominion of Egypt the nobility of Egypt retired themselves into the inland." The Moors moved to South and Western Europe, while northern Germanic tribes, were continuously descending south of the Baltic. [64]"The Barbarian hordes of great migration through Europe, had succumbed to the infection of the civilized settled communities," and in an attempt to abate this incursion, the Moors decided to join their kingdom by blood. This was the beginning of a long tradition of marrying the daughters of the Northern warriors. A marriage was arranged between [65]Pepin of the Northern Franks and Bertrade, daughter of the Count de Leon. Their son Charlemagne, united most of Europe from the North Sea to Italy and from the Atlantic Ocean to the Danube (Danubian) River for the first time.

Figure 25 a). Alfonso VII King of Leon and Castillia under the Moorish Empire of Spain 1126-1157.
b) Charles the great, Charlemagne & Carolus Magnus from the Coronation of the king, depicted in the Sacramentary of Charles the Bald (ca. 870) Paris, Bibliothèque nationale de France, ms. Latin 1141, A close examination of the Halos in many pieces appear to have been the impression of overgrown Afros.

With this new tradition, came a progressive transformation of language as Latin fused with the Slavic. This fusion manifested differently in different regions, and influenced modern Italian, Spanish, Portuguese, French and even English. [66]Although long before Charles the Great's time Rome had ceased to be the capital of the world, it still controlled the world's destinies, and the coronation of Charles in 800AD virtually meant the restoration of Rome to her old supremacy. [67]Charlemagne's greatest successes were in today's Germany, where in the course of a thirty years war against

[60]The journey-book of England. Berkshire (Derbyshire, Hampshire, Kent). By England 1840 pg. 125

[61] Titus Livius Patavinus, by Giacomo Filippo Tomasini, Andreas Frisius, 1670

[62] The Grove Encyclopedia of Islamic Art and Architecture, Volume 3 Jonathan M. Bloom, Sheila Blair Oxford University Press, 2009 – Art

[63] The History and Description of Africa: And of the Notable Things Therein Contained (Google eBook) Leo (Africanus), Robert Brown, John Pory Hakluyt Society, 1896 pg. 859

[64] Lafayette a life 1936 by Andreas latzko translated from German by E. W. Dickens 79

[65] A Geneology of South Worths by Samuel Gil

[66]A History of German Literature 6th Edition by J. G Robertson, published by William Blackwood and sons LTD Edingburg and London. 1949 pg 22-23

[67]Mckay, John, Hill and Buckler, A History of Western Society from antiquity to the enlightenment. Sixth edition. Houghton Miffin Company 1999 Pg 248

the Saxons, he slaughtered more than four thousand Saxons in one day. He conquered all of Europe and became its first emperor. [68]His personal influence was sufficiently powerful, to keep united a great nation composed of <u>so many different races</u>.

Spain And France

[69]After the Moors entered Spain and France, these became the most prominent European nations, and experienced the greatest periods of prosperity. But they were continuously at war with the Saxons. An account of one of the soldiers who died in this battle, was recorded in *the Song of Roland*. It is the **oldest** surviving major work of French literature. (Written in Old French)

[70]*Who holds Alferne, Kartagene, Garmalie, and Ethiope, a cursed land indeed; the Blackamoors from there are in his keep, Broad in the nose they are and flat in the ear, Fifty thousand and more in company. These canter forth with arrogance and heat, then they cry out the pagans' rallying-cheer; And Rolland says: "Martyrdom we'll receive; When Rolland sees those misbegotten men, who are more-black than ink is on the pen, With no part, White, only their teeth except...*

[71]A Blackamoor, or moor is defined as a Negro or a very dark person and *Schwartz* is German for Black, so Schwarzenegger is the German translation for a Black Niger or Blackamoor. Their rich dark complexion was so distinctive, that they could claim to have been Gods. For many centuries, this myth spread readily through the organism of the Catholic church, through superfluous iconography and painted images which reinforced this idea of a divine class in distinct contrast to the common subjects. This is the basis for the hatred of Catholics, Italians and Irish, as they remained a powerful force against the Aryans for many centuries.

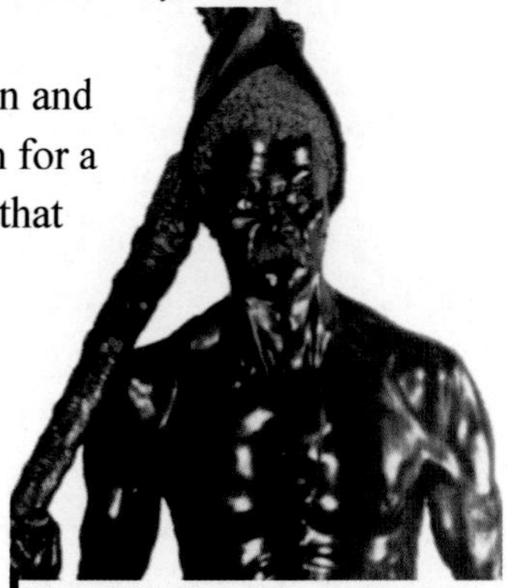

Figure 26 The Saracen/Moorish Army outside Paris, 730-32 AD, by Julius Schnorr von Carolsfeld, 1822-27

Figure 27 "A moor, statue in ebony (Ca'Rezzonico, Venice)" by Andrea Brustolon (1662-1732) A world History of Art by Gina Pischel 1968 p481

---

[68] The Life of Alfred the Great Reinhold Pauli, Paulus Orosius, Benjamin Thorpe, G. Bell & sons, 1893 World history- 582 pg1

[69] The Jews and Moors in Spain Joseph Krauskopf M. Berkowitz & Company, 1886. This is the best account of the history of Spain and the invasion from the records of Arabians and the comprehensive research of this author. P228

[70] The Song of Roland: Done into English, in the Original Measure Dutton, 1920 Pg. 63

[71] A Dictionary of the English Language: Compiled for the Use of Common Schools in the United States Noah Webster George Goodwin, 1817

31

Figure 28 1794 Anville Map of the Western Roman Empire

[72]By the year 1095 the whole of Moorish Spain was in the hands of the Moors, forming an integral part of a vast empire whose center of gravity was Morocco, and whose southern limit was in Senegal. [73]From the 12th to the 13th centuries, the chief trading center and one of the liveliest in the entire world, was the prosperous island city of Kiliwa. Located on the coast of Tanzania, Kiliwa received goods from the interior and exchanged them for products from foreign lands. Great Zimbabwe was also a flourishing civilization around this time, [74]At its peak the city appears to have been inhabited by 20,000 people… constructed with tightly fitted granite slabs, without mortar "(rather like the castles walls of medieval Europe)." In case you missed the implication of this comparison, here is what this means. Many of the castles which were built *later* throughout Europe, employed the very same construction techniques as was initially used to build Great Zimbabwe, which died out at the time when the castles were being built in Europe. By the same people, who were migrating North at this time.

At the end of the 12th century, Timbuktu in Mali, was the center of wealth and scholarship. Scholars from Persia, Cairo and Baghdad journeyed for months across the sands of the Sahara to study there. It is estimated that, [75]over 25,000 students attended the University of Timbuktu. The Ahmed Baba Research Center housed the largest collection of sacred manuscripts. There were an estimated 700,000 manuscripts throughout private collections in Timbuktu. Some of these may have been brought over from the library of Alexandria in Egypt by Senegalese Wolof peoples, whose [76]philosophy of justice is identical to the Egyptian model… and indeed the similarity seems to be borne out even at the level of language." Some aspects of Wolof language also have similarities to creole. [77]Some of the material covered in the texts ranged from history, to Geography, astronomy, medicine and law; writings which date back in some cases as far as the 13th century," but most probably significantly earlier. Researchers for the Encyclopedia Britannica in 1903, determined that, [78]"tradition and history (were) in accord in representing the most ancient inhabitants of the oases to have been the Berauna, a name under which the

[72] The Rise of the Spanish Empire in the Old World and in the New, Volume 1 by Roger Bigelow Merriman Macmillan, 1918 page 14-23

[73] Davidson, Basil: African Kingdoms, Time Life Books Collection (The Great Ages of Man.) 1978 pg. 29

[74] Mysteries of History by Robert Stewart National Geographic Washington DC 2003 pg80

[75] Reclaiming the Ancient Manuscripts of Timbuktu by Chris Rainier for National Geographic News May 27, 2003

[76] Hensley, Travis Doctoral research: Exploring African law and ancient Egypt loc blog August 2017

[77] BBC News. Mali conflict: Timbuktu manuscripts destroyed 6/28/2015 http://www.bbc.com/news/world

[78] The Encyclopedia Britannica: A-ZYM Day Otis Kellogg, Thomas Spencer Baynes, William Robertson Smith Werner, 1903 volume(F)Fezzan pg. 129-130

Arabs group the Negros of Bornu as well as Tembu. The oldest dynasty of the Berauna was that of the Nesur, originally from Sudan. Its kings reigned at traghen, were long in power until... A sheriff of Morocco, Sid-el-Montesser-uld Mohamed, being elected sultan, founded the dynasty of Uled Mohammed which reigned for about 550 years," until 1811.

[79]Nigrita and the country of the Garamante seem, for the most part, to have been peopled at first from Egypt and Ethiopia...some of the most perfect Egyptian mummies now remaining incline us to think, that the features of the present Negroes; is a proof that the latter must have originally been related to the former. The languages therefore spoken in these regions, bore a great affinity at first to the Egyptian, Arabic, and Ethiopic... [80]The Berauna (or Bornu) above mentioned were identical with the Garamantes, so that it becomes almost a matter of certainty that from a very ancient date, a Negro civilization prevailed over the northern Sahara; and that this was far advanced for its time is shown by the remains of remarkable hydraulic works, by tombs of distinct character, and by rock sculptures which record the chief facts of their history." Early *European* explorers considered Fezzan a mixed people of [81]"Teda, Bornu, Tuareg, Berber and Arab who varied in color from Black to pure White, but with features and woolly hair of Negroes."

During the dark ages in Europe, the Malian Empire of West Africa, founded by Sundiata Keita, became renowned for the wealth of its rulers, especially Mansa Musa I, the wealthiest man alive then and in the ranks of all time. [82]Under Musa, Mali became one of the largest empires in the world and Tombouctou a major commercial city. His predecessors had begun expeditions, west of the Atlantic and colonized the Amharicas. The people around the Black Sea, the Armenians and Turks, joined the North African Moors and together became the Ottomans. [83]The ancient Nubians established a system of geometry including early versions of sun clocks and used a trigonometric methodology. Throughout their history Egyptians and Ethiopians and the Incas civilization from (1200-1535) referred to themselves as children of the sun.

Figure 29 Miniature of knights. (with the Penhalurik banner) Bibliotheque Nationale, Paris. Mckay, etal History of Western Society from antiquity to the enlightenment. Sixth edition. Houghton Miffin Company 1999 Pg299

Germany/Prussia

Prussia was already home to many Blacks since the arrival of Saint Maurice and the Ethiopian soldiers. But by the thirteenth century, this area became an established trading port. [84]The ancient towns of this land contain many curious and interesting relics of the old trading companies. At Riga is Schwartzhaupter Haus, (Black-heads house) erected about 1200AD, a

[79] An Universal History: From the Earliest Accounts to the Present Time, Part 1, Volume 16 page174 Princeton University George Sale, George Psalmanazar, Archibald Bower, George Shelvocke, John Campbell, John Swinton C. Bathurst, **1780**
[80] ibid
[81] The History of the Revolutions in the Empire of Morocco: Upon the Death of the Late Emperor Muley Ishmael; Being a Most Exact Journal of what Happen'd in Those Parts in the Last and Part of the Present Year. With Observations, Natural, Moral and Political, Relating to that Country and People. By John Braithwaite, James and John Knapton, Arthur Bettesworth, 1729 Pg.285
[82] Webster's new explorer desk encyclopedia 2003 pg. 830 Musa Emperor of Mali from 1307/ 1324
[83] The Journal of Egyptian Archaeology. Vol. 84, 1998 Gnomons at Meroë and Early Trigonometry. pg. 171
[84] Two Thousand Years of Gild Life: An Outline of the History and Development of the Gild System from Early Times, with Special Reference to Its Application to Trade and Industry; Together with a Full Account of the Gilds and Trading Companies of Kingston-upon-Hull, from the 14th to the 18th Century Joseph Malet Lambert A. Brown and sons; [etc., etc.,], 1891 - Guilds – pg154

brotherhood of unmarried merchants called Black-heads, from their patron saint, St. Mauritius. This is the background for the institution of many Black Statues and iconography, including the statute of Saint Maurice and the Black Madonna's which adorned the churches. As they moved into Rome, France, North Africa, Ireland and England [85][86]the wealthiest families, like the Tucher, Reiter, Durer and Holper were featured as Moors on their coat of arms. [87]Penhalurik, qual. Pen-halou-rick (head of the Rich Moors.)

England, Spain and Portugal

In 1300, [88]"King Edward I, the Black king of Wales," settled in Scotland. Edward II was crowned King of France from 1337 and in 1356 and the Black Prince defeated his French rivals. Around the same time, Ivan I became grand Duke of Russia and named his capital 'Moor'sCo,'

Figure 30 Edward_III_of_England_(Order_of_the_Garter)

Of his Perſonage and Conditions.

HE was tall of ſtature, higher then ordinary men by head and ſhoulders, and thereof called *Longſhank*; of a ſwarthy complexion, ſtrong of body, but lean; of a comely favour; his eyes in his anger ſparkling like fire; the hair of his head black and curled.

Precisely at the height of prominence in Africa, and the Inca renaissance in Mexico, this new royal aristocratic class arrived in Europe with names like *Edward or Hugh the Black,* [89]James Stuart the Black Knight, Ludovico Sforza the moor, or Giovanni Moro. The new immigrants succumbed to plagues from their encounter with European diseases which decimated large numbers of their population. This event was memorialized for centuries as the Black Death. But after centuries of cohabitation new vernacular languages began to develop, which represented the offspring of the particular group of foreigners and their merger with the Saxons. At this time, [90]grammar teaching meant the teaching of Latin Grammar. All the valuable books extant in all the vernacular dialects of Europe, would hardly have filled a single shelf. England did not yet possess Shakespeare's plays, nor France Montaigne's Essays, nor

---

[85] A Short View of the Families of the Scottish Nobility: Their Titles, Marriages, Issue, Descents; To which are Added, a List of All Those Peers Who Have Served in Parliament Since the Union; By Mr. Salmon by Nathaniel Salmon W. Owen, 1759 pg87 moor's head Nuremburg

[86] The Peerage of Ireland: A Genealogical and Historical Account of All the Peers of that Kingdom; Their Descents, Collateral Branches, Births, Marriages, and Issue ... with Paternal Coats of Arms, Crests, Supporters, and Mottoes ... Some Account of the Antient Kings, &c, Volume 2 by Edward Kimber, John Almon, 1768 pages 4,121,179, 210.

[87] Patronymica Cornu-Britannica: or, The etymology of Cornish surnames by Richard Stephen Charnock Longmans, Green, Reader and Dyer, 1870 pg. 85

Observations on the Antiquities Historical and Monumental of the County of Cornwall (etc.)-Oxford, W. Jackson 1754 by William Borlase (Cornish English vocabulary) 402

[88] Chronicle of the Kings of England: With Additions Richard Baker 1670 pg102

[89] The history of Scotland, from the year 1423 until the year 1542: Containing the lives and reigns of James the I. the to the V. With several memorials of state, during the reigns of James VI. and Charls V. William Drummond g.47 Printed by H. Hills, for R. Tomlins and himself, 1655

[90] Early schools and school-books of New England by George Emery Littlefield, Club of Odd Volumes The Club of Odd Volumes, 1545 pg. 231-232

Figure 31 William Tyndale 1494-1536

Spain Don Quixote. It was more than a century before William Tyndale (1494-1536) tried to enlighten the masses of Saxon subjects, by translating the bible to English. Although he was executed, his efforts to educate them, stirred the curiosity of the succeeding generation of Angelized-Saxons. Still Latin remained the main literary language in Europe until the Revolutions, and the campaigns for nationalization.

The new diverse population began a process of integration which led to an amalgamation of languages now considered "Germanic;" but the fact is, the English or German languages, were still fluid. They did not receive an official form until the mid-19th century. The so-called Pidgin Senegalese clearly resembles an early stage of English.

Figure 32 a) Unknown man by Jan Mostaert (1475-1555)
b) Charles V by Titian (1490-1576)

By the [91]"fifteenth century, sizeable numbers of Blacks entered Europe especially Spain and Portugal, but around 1492, [92]Ferdinand drove seven hundred thousand Moorish families out of Spain, to the great impoverishment and depopulation of that kingdom. Once the Moors were overthrown, the Spanish empire soon began to decline. After the friction in Spain the Moors, begun to move into Portugal.

Hence forth Portugal one of the newest homes of the Moorish refuges took up the mantle to continue trade and navigation of the known world.

There is a record of extensive correspondence between Afonso I, king of the Kongo with the Portuguese written in Portuguese around the early 1500s. The new Spanish monarchy in desperate need to find the source of economic power, which the vanquished Moors had held, set out in search of the gold. At first, they were fooled into thinking that the world was flat and that only those with magical powers could cross the oceans. It wasn't until one of the [93]"forgotten figures in American history, a Moorish Negro named Esteban…" led the Spanish across the ocean, that this myth was finally dispelled. Esteban spoke many languages including the dialects of the native tribes and led the Spanish into the bustling Mexican empire. By the time that Cortes arrived in the capital city of Tenochtitlan in 1519, it was already one of the largest cities in the world, with a population of 150,000 to 300,000 people. Upon seeing the capital for the first time, Cortes wrote: "The city itself is as large as Seville or Cordova… Every kind of merchandise in every land is for sale there…"

After encountering the Spanish, a plague of smallpox took hold of Tenochtitlan, killing hundreds of the citizens. Meanwhile, the Spaniards returned to take advantage of their destruction. We have been told that they brought in thousands of Africans to settle in the new world, but it is now obvious that they had already been there.

---

[91]Mckay, John, Hill and Buckler, A History of Western Society from antiquity to the enlightenment. Sixth edition. Houghton Miffin Company 1999 Pg435-436
[92] Nicholas Machiavelli. The works of Nicholas Machiavelli
[93] Alistair Cooke's America, Alfred A knopf INc, New York 1973 Borzoi Books p37

[94] *The cruelties of the Spanish tyrant, excelled those of Phalaris and Nero. He massacred above a hundred rich Christian merchants among the Moors, only to invade their effects. He miserably put to death twenty million people in the Indies, to enjoy their estates and boasts of having shed the Blood of above eighteen thousand poor innocent creatures by the hand of the publick executioners.*

Figure 33a) Maasai women from Arusha Tanzania in 2015, Some of their words are a kin to Latin, Spanish and Portuguese. Once upon a time their jewlry was mainly gold, today they use plastic beads.
b) Don Fransico De la robe and his sons Pedro and Domingo by Andres Sanchez Gallque 1590

The Spanish robbed and killed the Moors and took over their possessions in the New World. But even though they were successful at taking over many ancient civilizations, they never attained the political acuity to retain hold of these nations once they invaded them. The source of wealth and economic survival remained elusive. The Guinea company which was founded in 1588, received a charter from Charles I in England, and Guinean soldiers began immigrating into England, defeating the Spanish Armada a fleet of over 130 ships. By 1607, the Spanish empire was totally bankrupt.

Figure 34 Left)Painting at king's Fountain in Lisbon Portugal. 1570-1590
Top) Painting of Portuguese Orchestra 1520

---

[94] A new voyage to Italy: with curious observations on several other countries, as: Germany, Switzerland, Savoy, Geneva, Flanders, and Holland; together with useful instructions for those who shall travel thither, Volume 1, Part 1 Maximilien Misson inted for R. Bonwicke, 1714 pg. 534

Italy

Years after the fall of Italy a new resurgence of Moorish migrants returned to recapture the country and inaugurated the renaissance of the fourteenth century.[95]In Renaissance Spain and Italy, Black performers, dancers and actors in courtly dramas and musicians, sometimes made up entire orchestras. [96]Ludovico Sforza the   moor, was regent of Milan and the Maurus family had ruled Venice since the twelfth century and retained hereditary rule through Doges like Cristoforo and Giovanni Moro. The characteristics of the kings and aristocracy, the buildings they erected, and the trajectory of development, make it incontestable, that Africans were largely responsible for raising the pillars of civilization in Europe. The extant potraits have suffered extreme alterations, but the features still indicate significant admixture within the ranks of the aristocracy.

Figure 35 a) Maria_de_Medici_by_Frans_Pourbus_or_Scipione_Pulzone b) Angelo_Bronzino_medici c) Cosimo I de Medici grand duke of Tuscany in armor by Agnolo Bronzino 1545 housed at the Art Gallery of New South Wales Foundation Purchase 1996 - d) Portrait of Maria Salviati de' Medici mother of Cosimo I (1519-1574), little girl was painted over until the 20th century Walters_museum37596 e) Alessandro de Medici.

Figure 36 Antonio Emanuele Funta by Francesco Capole 1608. At Saint Maria Baptistry, Rome. Black Africans in Renaissance Europe. Edited by Thomas Foster Earle K.J. Lowe Cambridge University Press.

Africans returned from the encroaching Sahara and within a generation, Rome regained its status as the axis of the world. The Medici's sponsored many artists built and governed the Vatican with the creation of cathedrals and a banking system which furthered the expansion of the Catholic Church. Popes Leo X, Clement VII, Pius IV, and Leo XI were descendants of the Medici's'. The Medici's continued the tradition of tying their nations together through marriage. One daughter Catherine Medici (1519-1589) became queen of France after marrying King Henry II and three of her sons inherited thrones in other parts of Europe. Cosimo Medici's granddaughter Marie, became queen of France when she married Henry IV in 1600. Their son Louis XIII ruled for three decades from 1610-43.

---

[95] (A. C. DE. C. M Saunders A Social History of Black slaves in and freedmen in Portugal, 1441-1555 NY: Cambridge University Press 1982), pp.59, 62,88 176-179.) 436.

[96] The history of England, Volume 1 Rapin de Thoyras (Paul, M.) J. and P. Knapton, 1743 pg717

The Setting Sun

*Figure 37 **a)** Othello by William Mulready (Irish, 1786-1863) the collection of Tate Britain **b)** teloe Desdémona by Antonio Muñoz Degraín **c)** 1943 production of Othello starring Paul Robeson and Uta Hagen*

England's initial Brexit, provided the model for the general disintegration and eventual collapse of all monarchical power throughout Europe. The general atmosphere in the fifteenth century, was one of enlightenment and awakening among the common people. [97]"The war of the pen, preceded the war of the sword," with writings like, Luther's Ninety-Five Theses, published in 1518 and that of other theologians, like Calvin, which attacked the authority of the Roman Catholic Church. But when Henry VIII, king of England decided to break away from the church, this served to legitimize all other renegade movements and opened the door for increased protestant ideology throughout Europe. [98]"By 1534 Parliament stopped all payments to Rome and transferred all papal powers to the king, who became the supreme head of the church of England. Henry kept all the money which would have been sent to Rome, in order to sustain his kingdom and confiscated all church property. At this time, the monasteries had their property seized, and Catholic priests were under persecution.

Queen Elizabeth (1558-1603) choose the course of compromise between the conservatives who preferred the ancient structure and the Protestants who demanded change; but the country soon began to feel the financial strains of isolation. She managed to circumvent her reliance on the Moors, by creating a new alliance directly with the Guineans. The Guinean company founded in 1588, cut out the Moorish middle men and created a new powerful military and economic alliance, through direct trade of gold and other essential resources. After Elizabeth's death, James I (1566-1625) became King of England in 1603. [99]King James was well-proportioned and stately in his person, and of a swarthy (dark) complexion.

The earliest writings in the native tongue, reveal the issues of greatest interest and most popular day to day discussions. Writers like William Shakespeare (1564-1616), and Miguel Cervantes (1547-1616) author of Don Quixote, provide a glimpse into these times. Their work identifies the prevalent and powerful position of Moors like, Robert Ridolfi, a wealthy Florentine banker, who was the agent for the Pope in London. Shakespeare's Moor (renamed-Merchant) from Venice, dramatized these wealthy merchants from Venice.

From 1618 to 1648 the monarchs all over Europe were entangled in a Thirty Years' War, which was being fought in central Europe. In France Louis XIII son of the Medici's ruled for three decades from 1610-43, while in England, King James ruled until 1625. The spread of literacy came with dissent and, so

---

[97] Oliver Cromwell Popular History. Rev. M. Russell. D. M. Mac Lelland Book Co. New York 1910 p83

[98] The Columbia Encyclopedia HenryVIII 936

[99]A New & full, Critical, Biographical, & Geographical History of Scotland: containing the history of the succession of their kings from Robert Bruce, to the present time. With a geographical description of the several counties... together with an appendix... and a map of each county in Scotland, William Duff Printed for the author, 1749 pg.128

in 1611 James published the King James Bible. The publication of the Bible provided the legitimacy for the kings' claims of divine birth because he was the provider of the scriptures. But it was evident that the growing tensions between the wealthy *foreigners* and the commoners would eventually lead to total disintegration. Thus, King James set out to find new territory, and in 1607 a group sailed from London with 105 men, to found Jamestown, named after the king.

In 1619, he invited a vessel of Black males from Africa to increase his new settlement. One of these Black men Anthony Johnson, [100]"acquired considerable land." The following year, English ladies were brought in from England, most probably as the bounty for the new settlers and by 1624 William Tucker, the first African American was born. This was the beginning of Virginia, the first successful settlement in America. The founders of New England attempted from the start to carefully select those who were permitted to become settlers. John White a member of the Massachusetts Bay Company, discussed the objectives of the colonists:

Figure 38 John White

[101]A State that intends to draw out a colony for the inhabiting of another country, must look at the mother and the daughter... and consequently must allow to her such a proportion of able men as may bee sufficient to make the frame of that new body; As good governors, able ministers, physitians, souldiers, school masters, mariners, and mechanicks of all sorts... because the first fashioning of a politicke body is a harder task then the ordering of that which is already framed. When the frame of the body is thus formed the bulk may be filled up with persons of less use and activity. False stones in a foundation ruine the whole building.

This underscores the fact that Africans were deliberately sort after for the laying of the foundation of American society, not because of a perceived inferiority, but quite the contrary. [102]Before the sixteenth century "discoveries" of the non-European world, Europeans (Caucasians) had little concrete knowledge of Africans and their cultures." But Spanish revolutionaries had experienced more than five hundred years of intimate intercourse. They succeeded in evicting the Moors from Spain and tried to undermine them everywhere else. In their quest to illuminate the dark secrets of the Blacks; they invited Walter Raleigh from England to visit Guinea. There he discovered that the general population lived in the same degree of poverty as the Brutish commoner. This challenged the concept of "high birth" which once elevated the distinct features of the nobility. Raleigh realized that nobility was related to wealth and not ancestry. For this discovery, he was sentenced to twelve years in prison, where he wrote the first volume of his 'History of the World.' Two years later, King James had him executed; but once the lie was exposed, the damage was done. His writings may not be completely reliable, since they were produced during the oppressive reign of King James; but his oral accounts must have been circulated.

Then, in 1624 England declared war on Spain, meanwhile an increased demand for soldiers forced the monarchy to open the knighthood to more commoners. After James died, his son Charles I (1600-1649) took the throne and married [103]the daughter of France, a Roman Catholic, Henrietta Maria,

[100] The Negro Church in America by E. Franklin Frazier, Schocken Books. New York. 1968 pg 20

[101] John White "The Planters Plea, or The Grounds of Plantations Examined..." [London 1630], in Force, ed., Tracts. II, 19-20, 45" Diamond, Sigmund, Sellers, Charles. The creation of society in the New World. The Berkeley Series in American History The recruitment of a population Chapter III pg. 42.

[102] Mckay, John, Hill and Buckler, A History of Western Society from antiquity to the enlightenment. Sixth edition. Houghton Miffin Company 1999 Pg435-436

[103] Oliver Cromwell Popular History. Rev. M. Russell. D. M. Mac Lelland Book Co. New York 1910 69-70

who brought with her a train of priests and spiritual dependents. The marriage was probably an act of economic desperation, and an attempt to reassert the alliance between the Holy See and England. It served instead, as a wedge between the people and the monarchy and laid the foundation for Oliver Cromwell (1599–1658) a member of the <u>House of Commons,</u> to assemble forces against the crown.

Figure 39 Fresco depicting a tournament of knights. "Hall of Pisanello" Ducal Palace, Mantua Italy, (1433) from archives of realhistoryww.com

[104]"The outcry of abuse from the lowest classes regarding the increase of popery and the arrival of foreign troops… divided the country into two great bodies. The roundheads and the Cavaliers. The Roundheads received their name from the custom of wearing their hair, cut close around their heads, with so many little peaks, that the name roundhead became the scornful term, given to the whole parliament party, whose army marched out as if they had been sent out only after their hair had grown two or three years after."

Many of these overgrown round heads represent "afros" which were later changed into Halos. In 1625 full bottom wigs became a custom, which further distinguished the members of parliament as either Whigs or Tories. These foreign troops came from Africa. At this time [105]the King of Benin had the capability to prepare 20,000 men for war, per day and, if need be, 180,000, and because of this he had great influence among all the surrounding peoples… His authority stretched over many cities, towns and villages. There was no King thereabouts who, was in the possession of so many beautiful cities and towns, his equal. [106]Huge earthworks surrounded Benin, with inner defense measuring 17 meters from the bottom of the ditch to the top of the bank, which would have taken many man hours to build.

Cromwell's' small cavalry crushed the king's army, probably with the aid of the biological weapons which preceded his attack. These had the historic success of wiping out populations ahead of invasion, just as the Justinian Plague came before the fall of Rome, and Cortez before the Mexicans. [107]The first deaths occurred in a house in Westminster, other accounts say with greater precision in Long Acre, and that the first sufferers were these foreigners. The first great epidemic of the 17th century was the terrible destructive one of 1603. It lingered for some years, and even in 1609 the mortality was considerable. The epidemic of 1636 was less destructive, but remarkable for its long continuance, considerable mortality being recorded every year up to 1647. The period, of Commonwealth when Cromwell assumed power, was practically exempt. "The *Commonwealth*" (suggests a distribution of crown lands to the common people).

In [108]the Battle of Marston Moor, Cromwell says that [109]"despite Plagues, of war and fire, false Canaanites Swarm the land, the city is a lay stall full of mire and ought again to be new purged with fire." Cromwell speaks of a desperate need to *purge* the land of these swarms of Canaanites; because the "*Black* plague" as it is still remembered, was not enough to purge Blacks from England.

---

[104] Ibid: 83-84

[105] Dapper, Olfert Nauwkeurige Beschrijvinge der Afrikaansche Gewesten (Description of Africa), **1668**

[106] Past worlds the Times Atlas of Archeaology edited by Chris Scarre pg. 250

[107] An Account of the Great Plague of London in the Year 1665: Now First Printed from the British Museum Sloane Ms. 349, for the Epidemiological Society of London XI-XII William Boghurst Shaw, 1894 Loimographia,

[108] Pope, Alexander The works of William Shakespeare, 1861 volume 1 pg. 237, 240 & lxxix. Act five, scene two

[109] Poems on the affairs of the state in the time of Oliver Cromwell.pg383 to 399

Difcord and Care, which do diftract him here,
In Durance take their leave, and come not there.
Falfe Friends and Flatterers then take laft adieu,
Who often fwore how faithful and how true,
Things their difhoneft Bofoms never knew.
Thefe, like the Swallows, in cold Weather fly;
A Summer's Fortune only draws them nigh.
Flatt'rers a fort of fatal Suckers be,
Which draw the Sap till they deftroy the Tree.
Fair Virtue to their Opticks when they bring,
Seems a deform'd and antiquated thing.
Vice they commend, whilft Virtue is defpis'd;
The Blackeft by thefe *Negroes* moft are pris'd.
Thefe Slaves to Vice do hug fo hard and long,
Till like the o'er-fond Ape they kill their Young.
Ambition in the Mind's a feverifh Thirft,
Which is by drinking drier than at firft;
And thefe will feed the Humor till it burft.
When Parafites the Arbiters are made,
They'l place the Garland on a *Bedlam's* Head.
Riot, Excefs, and Pleafure car' the Day,
And Luft (the worft of Tyrants) bears the fway,
At whofe black Throne they blind *Allegiance* pay.
Morofe and dull they do account the Grave;
And the meek Man, fit only for a Slave:

The legend of Robin Hood and his band of thieves, was the bedtime story of the day and fits perfectly with Oliver Cromwell. After he became the supreme ruler, the country's foreign alliances, including the French, refused to do business with the British, so the wealthy were most probably being robbed to help the poor. After Cromwell's death, they were forced to invite Charles II back, and he received Tangier, as part of the portion of his wife, Catherine of Portugal.

In 1665 there was a resurgence of the plague. The great plague of London spread rapidly leaving a death toll of 7,000 a week from the 14th of September. Then in 1666 the Great Fire of London, consumed 13,200 houses and 87 churches. The people fleeing London in the 17th century were not the common folk, but the wealthy royals and their armies, the so-called *foreigners*. They transplanted themselves in the New World to begin anew and it is no wonder why they sought out Africans. In 1681 a colony of about three thousand settled on the banks of the Delaware and within years settlers came in large numbers. Those who fled to the tiny islands of the Caribbean were spared simply because the islands were smaller and more easily defendable. Hundreds of last names on the islands are connected to royalist soldiers, clergy and merchants. St. Lucians fought fourteen wars against the British and French, using bamboo pipes in place of canons.

Then in 1682 another group planted a colony at the Gulf of Mexico and named it Louisiana after the King of France, Louis XIV, the *Sun King*. As the population of commoners attained equal status, the civil wars gradually ceased there; and [110]in 1688 Parliament, had been led by certain extreme acts of James II, to draw up the Declaration of Right, which defined the relation between the king and his subjects. This forerunner to John Locke's social contract, established the governing powers of the country.

---

[110] The English Bill of Rights 1689.

> Considering that Englishmen have invaded every country in the world for commercial and industrial purposes, it is unreasonable and ungenerous on their part to complain about the migration of foreign labourers hither. But for the influx of foreigners in times past, England would not have secured her manufacturing supremacy. It must not be forgotten that some of our most profitable industries were taught us by foreigners. Nor does the influence which foreigners have exerted in the development of British manufactures belong exclusively to the period of 'ancient history.' Our chief manufacture, namely, that of iron and steel, still owes much to them. Both of our two new centres of this great industry—Middlesborough and Barrow-in-Furness—have been, practically, the creation of foreigners, the late Mr. Bolckow having been the founder of the former, art and science, as well as in industry, we have been laid under a heavy debt of gratitude to foreigners. The grand cathedrals of which we boast were largely the work of foreign stonemasons, We owe even our House of Commons to a foreigner.
>
> It is manifestly unreasonable, therefore, to denounce foreigners as intruders upon British soil. Still it is unfortunate that in one great industry, namely, seamanship, foreigners [111]should preponderate over Englishmen.

After the monarchy was overthrown in England, aggressive efforts towards nationalization, led to a series of repressive laws. Some Nobles fled across the Atlantic to America, others fled North and established Prussia by 1700, but on their heels, were the same illuminators, [112]"imported from England to Germany, before the middle of the eighteenth century," through writings like Joseph Butler's Analogy of Religion in 1736. The rapidly expanding population of Germanic people, weakened the military opposition of the Old Regime, and their defeat was captured by orchestras throughout the region, in the somber and deeply depressed music of composers of the day. Johann Sebastian Bach (1685-1750) a famous German composer who [113]was... rather short in stature, with black hair and eyes and a brown complexion, Joseph Bologne, Chevalier de Saint-Georges (1745-1799) a famous fencer, and violinist, and the conductor of the leading symphony orchestra in Paris. He became a colonel of the Légion St.-Georges, during the French Revolution, an all-Black regiment in Europe and Ignatius Sancho (1729-1780), a British composer, actor, writer.

Figure 40 a) Johann Sebastian Bach b) Chevalier de Saint-Georges c) Ignatius Sancho

---

[111] A wizard's wandering from China to Peru. By John Watkins Holden FSS 1885

[112] Outlines of German Literature by Joseph Gostwick & Robert Harrison Holt & Williams F. W. Christern 1873 p.vii

[113] The Present State of Music In Germany, The Netherlands, And United Provinces. Or the Journal of a Tour Through Those Countries, Undertaken to Collect Materials for A General History of Music: In Two Volumes, Volume 2 Charles Burney, Becket, 1775 pg.271

Figure 41 Many of the portraits which were not destroyed were simply reclassified as African kings. These say adoration of the Magi or adoration of Kings, they illustrate the presence of blacks in the highest class.

By 1746 a new law forbade the wearing of Tartans, the distinctive headdress of the Moorish Kings. John Milton protested the entire idea of a king, which meant they were still subjects, [114]"fitter to be led back into their old servitude." In England the practice of marrying foreign royals, which had maintained the Negro strain for centuries, was abolished in 1770, when Parliament passed the Royal marriage act, to prohibit the English monarchy from marring foreigners. King George III (1738-1820) of England and Queen Charlotte, [115]With features, as conspicuously Negroid, directly descended from Margarita de Castro y Sousa, the Black Portuguese Royal House, (they had fifteen children) and these were the last branch of monarchs with the old negro strain. ....

At this time the new British powers, began to set sail throughout the world to disrupt the trading economy of the Ottomans. They successfully invaded India and other parts of Asia and blocked the importation of food from the African farmers. It is estimated that between 1770 and 1790 ten million people died from wide spread famine in India. This may have been the first man made famine in World history, but it set a precedent and legacy which other Aryan leaders tried to surpass. In years to come tens of millions of people would be murdered this way ,too many to account for here.

Figure 42 Charles VI, Holy Roman Emperor and his family by Martin Van Meytens 1675-1770

At this time Austrian [116]Emperor Charles VI of a middle stature, moderately fat, of a hale, swarthy, a brisk eye and thick lips; the latter being the *distinguishing mark* of the Austrian family, was one of the Monarchs of the still oppressed regions of Austria, who welcomed the fleeing nobles, to maintain monarchical solidarity. But in Russia, [117]Peter the Great (1682-1725), moved the capital from Moors'co to St. Petersburg in 1703... because he "desired with great aid to drive the Ottomans from Europe; and after his death the crown passed to female heirs who married Germans and German influence greatly increased." From this point on, the monarchies as the country became more Germanized.

[114] Milton, John, Kearsley, G, Eikonoklastes: In Answer to a Book Intittled Elkon Basilike, the Portraiture of his Sacred Majesty in his Solitudes and Sufferings 1770 page 271-272

[115] http://www.pbs.org/wgbh/pages/frontline/shows/secret/famous/royalfamily.htmlIN

[116] Modern History Or the Present State of All Nations, Volume 2 Thomas Salmon 1745 pg.62

[117] G. & C. Merriam Company, Webster's New International Dictionary of the English Language Based on the International Dictionary of 1890 and 1900: Now Completely Revised in All Departments, Including Also a Dictionary of Geography and Biography, Being the Latest Authentic Quarto Edition of the Merriam Series, Volume 1. G. & C. Merriam Company, 1926 (138)

Securing America

It was the Darkest of Nights

By the end of the eighteenth-century, most of the wealthy people, that emigrated from Europe, settled on the North-eastern coast of America. [118]The center of the population rested within eighteen miles of Balti-moor, north and west of Washington. South of Philadelphia the road was tolerable as far as Baltimore, but between Baltimore and Washington it meandered through forests. Regions like Ohio and Tennessee, were still wilderness. Of the whole United States, New England claimed to be the most civilized, but was still poor. There were no large-scale manufacturers, and the small population fed and clothed themselves through cottage industry (there was no commercial demand for slaves). The very first American doctors were from New England, and two of the signers were doctors from New Hampshire. When a smallpox epidemic broke out in Boston in 1721, Onesimus, introduced an inoculation procedure developed by Africans; and in Connecticut, a [119]Negro doctor Primus, owned a practice which was "considerable." The first hospital was built in Philadelphia, after the epidemic broke out there in 1751, and [120]"the elders of the African Church, Absalom Jones and Richard Allen, undertook to furnishing nurses..." Daniel Hale founded Provident Hospital in Chicago in 1891. He performed the first open-heart surgery in the world, there and a year later, the first ever medical journal was published by Miles Vandahurst Lynk of Tennessee; but hospitals were a luxury for some time, Jimmy Carter was the first president to be born in a hospital in 1924.

Property ownership was the basic requirement to political power. [121]Massachusetts, Connecticut and Rhode Island, all had Black Governors before changes began to take place in 1818, but Connecticut's vital records from 1700-1850, which would have provided an ethnographic portrait of the early governors have mysteriously vanished. Governor Oliver Wolcott, whose father was a colonial governor of Connecticut was described as [122]"being tall, *dark complexioned*, and dignified in appearance..." The family of Wentworth Cheswell (1746-1817) a politician from New Hampshire owned over fifty acres of land there, and he remained in public office until his death. Paul Cuffee (1759-1817), possessed several sail ships. Many [123]"Negroes were seamen on merchant ships, whaling boats and... more than half of all American seamen were Negroes." Absalom Boston (1785-1855) had an all Black

Figure 43 Paul Cuffe, Google Art Project Los Angeles Museum of Art.

[118] The United States in 1800 by Henry Adams, Man and Society Vol. 6 Gateway to great Books 1963 pg.328, -345

[119] Yankee Doodle, Green, pp. 118-19p57: The history of ancient Windsor, Connecticut, New York 1859 pp879 (from Connecticut Black Soldiers 1775-1783 by David White 1973. Pequot Press Chester Connecticut.)pg.12

[120] A Short Account of the Plague: Or Malignant fever, lately Prevalent in Philadephia: with a Statement on the proceedings that Took place in different parts of the United States. Mathew Carey 1794 p63

[121] Memoirs of Governor William Smith, of Virginia: His Political, Military, and Personal History by John W. Bell, William Smith Moss engraving Company, 1891 pg 422

[122] Know the Signers of the Declaration of Independence by, George Ross 1963 US

[123] A Pictorial History of Black Americans, 5th revised edition by Langston Hughes, Milton Meltzer, and C. Eric Lincoln. Crown Publishers New York 1983 p 68

crew on his whale ship the Industry. Lewis Temple, was the blacksmith who invented the universal whale iron and Prince Hall (1735-1807) a contemporary of Benjamin Banneker, founded the Boston Freemasons. An exclusive worldwide society, with men like Angelo Soliman, [124]"tutor to Vienna's richest and most eminent aristocrats." Benjamin F was also the founder of a secret society in Pennsylvania. Many politicians and wealthy citizens in Connecticut, like [125]Broteer Furro or Venture Smith (1729-?) were renamed or distorted.

Figure 44 Angelo Soliman Venice 1750

The most pressing issue was securing title to the country; so the African immigrants were mostly soldiers, farmers and skilled civil engineers, who came with a mission to build America. In 1729 a survey of the Mauritanian empire described the people there as [126]mostly horse-soldiers, ready to be sent on any immediate service. The palaces, were built entirely by Muley Ismael, and stand upon more ground than the city, and indeed are rather a city than a palace… The whole circumference of these Palaces may be near three or four miles, including several gardens, meadows… The inhabitants are divided into the Moors, who generally inhabit the sea coast, the Arabs who generally live in tents and inhabit the Plains. The Barebbers (Berbers), an ancient race of Moors who inhabit the Mountains and seem to be the original inhabitants of this country. The Jews who were chiefly drove from Spain and Portugal. And lastly the Negroes who make the greatest figure in this country. These six different people make up the subjects of the emperor of Morrocco… But the Negroes, are the Grand Cavaliers of this part.

These soldiers and aristocrats represented a significant number of the population; so that when Cripus Attukus was killed in the Boston Massacre in 1770, this set of the beginning of war. Benjamin Franklin proposed a union of the American colonies in 1774 and declared America an independent and

Figure 45 Moulay Abd-er-Rahman, Sultan of Morocco, surrounded by the Elite Black Guards and his principal officers. Painting from 1845

autonomous nation. The first Congress convened that September, with delegates from each of the thirteen English States. By December 6th, 1775, the new American congress renounced its ties to the new British

---

[124] Nettl, Paul Angelo Soliman-Friend of Mozart. Vol 7 No1 Clark Atlanta University 1946

[125] History of Middlesex County, Connecticut: With Biographical Sketches of Its Prominent Men. J.B. Beers & Company, 1884 pg. 405

[126] The History of the Revolutions in the Empire of Morocco: Upon the Death of the Late Emperor Muley Ishmael; Being a Most Exact Journal of what Happen'd in Those Parts in the Last and Part of the Present Year. With Observations, Natural, Moral and Political, Relating to that Country and People. By John Braithwaite, James and John Knapton, Arthur Bettesworth, 1729 Pg.285-350

Parliament, although they maintained loyalty to the king. In July 1776 the Americans declared their Independence. A few months later, in 1777 the new British government, under the House of commoners, hired 29,000 German soldiers. Like the Spanish pirates, they intended to raid the properties of the exiled aristocracy; so, the Americans appealed to the still reigning French aristocracy for military support.

Lafayette was sent by France to aid the Americans against the new English rulers. He arrived to find an abundance of open fields filled with [127]"fruits, which were "rotting... while in France men were starving!" In April 1778, he came within miles of the British vessels loaded with commoners and stood in awe of the English subjects who successfully liberated themselves and were now descending upon the world. In that moment, the view of the men fighting valiantly against the Americans, changed Lafayette's perspective of who the enemy actually was. He tried to turn some of the influential forces in the American army to his side, but without much success. Instead they placed him under investigation. Lafayette was forced to mute his doctrine, because it raised concern among most of the leaders, but Aaron Burr and Thomas Jefferson took the bait. He wrote to his wife to say: [128]"I could see that there was no possibility of winning them over to my view, and as it is the interest to the *common* cause that we should remain friends, I have roundly declared that everything I said was wrong." That August, Rhode Island formed an all-Black unit, to defeat the British in the Battle for Rhode Island.

When Lafayette returned to France in February 1779, "King Louis XVI received his insubordinate officer with a gracious smile." Somehow, he managed to convince the king that he was innocent; but this was only the beginning of his scheme to start the French Revolution. Meanwhile Jefferson also committed to the common cause, kept secret correspondence with the British general. He convinced the governor of Virginia to keep the four thousand surrendered British soldiers in Virginia, where he started to get acquainted with them. When discussion about moving the prisoners from Charlottesville, arose he protested. "Does every sentiment of humanity revolt against removing them into new situations." He sent a letter to Richard Henry, referring to government officials as his "secret enemies," and bypassed congress to [129]restore lines of communication directly with Lafayette. All of Jefferson's actions thereafter, indicate that he was trying to sabotage the American government; but his marriage to a Black woman and his Black offspring, blind sighted most of his contemporaries to his treasonous motives. Sally Hemmings, has been referred to as a slave for generations, but she bore Jefferson's children, travelled with him on his tour of Europe and enabled him to pass. For this slave, Jefferson spent lots of money on extravagant shopping in France. [130]"Jefferson had a superb sense of history and an exact understanding of his role in it. He preserved a legacy of over 25,000 letters from friends and acquaintances...These letters he indexed extending from 1783 to 1826. Still he *destroyed* what would have been among the most revealing of his life, his correspondence with his mother and his wife." Without Sally or Jefferson's testimony, it is impossible to dismiss the possibility that she was Jefferson's wife. Another possible alteration is Benjamin Banneker, whose versatile genius closely parallels Benjamin Franklin. Almost every piece of information available about either *Fr*ank or *B*ank appears posthumously. Banneker's home was burned after his funeral, and Franklin's "original" writings didn't surface until 1867, [131](when the first edition ever

---

[127] Lafayette a life 1936 by Andreas latzko translated from German by E. W. Dickens 167 48-77

[128] ibid 92

[129] Mapp, Alf J. A Strange Case of Mistaken Identity: Madison Books NY, London 1987 pg134 (Jefferson quotes)

[130] Thomas Jefferson an intimate history by Fawn H Brodie 1974 pg22

[131] The autobiography of Benjamin Franklin Art Type Edition. The world's popular classics Books Inc. New York.

printed from the original was given to the public) more than half a century after his death, coinciding with the rise of the Klu Klux Klan, the assassination of Abraham Lincoln and the new Jacksonian regime. [132]This was also around the time when the legend that Betsy Ross, designed the American flag was first told by her grandson in 1870. Before this time only the three colors were constant... It wasn't until 1912 that this current design was made official.

That June, after Jefferson was elected Governor of Virginia, British soldiers took Suffolk, Virginia's main military base. Congress demanded an explanation, but Jefferson replied, "though so near the scene he was not able to decide whether there were such or not." A year later, in April 1780 Lafayette and a crew of soldiers were sent again to America to help fight the British, they spent an entire year there without one shot being fired at the enemy. This reluctance to open fire on the British, essentially made him a hero because his hesitation by happenstance brought victory. The British general Cornwallis and his men were forced out of Yorktown, and Lafayette's hesitation was considered tactful and strategic. Jefferson then requested and was granted 20,000 men, horses and other items for military purposes, ahead of a suspected British invasion, in South Carolina. But in September when the generals called for help, Jefferson sent an unarmed militia to defend their post in South Carolina. General Gates, demanded an account of the supplies that were sent to him; but Jefferson responded with a taunting message, "look forward to much difficulty and a perplexed department."

Figure 45 Photo of aged John Hanson probably in his 90s in the mid-1830s, Daguerreotype by Augustus Washington a Blackman from Connecticut, who owned one of few early studios in the nation at this time, located on Main St in Hartford.

Jefferson's treason was finally apparent, in June of 1781, after a British fleet entered the Chesapeake under his watch and managed to build forts in Suffolk without any resistance. The congress of equal members, recognized a need for a central leader and separate territory which would serve as the headquarters for the entire nation. They elected John Hanson, from Frederick County Maryland, the [133]"first "President of the United States." The first order of business was an investigation into Jefferson's sabotage. He was replaced, with Thomas Nelson and the military then stationed in New England was called to New York.

[134]Before 1781 New England infantry was so integrated, that the Black soldier, was rarely distinguishable from the White. But after these incidents, Massachusetts and Connecticut, after Rhode Island's 1778 model, formed all Black Regiments also. The Massachusetts unit was called the "Bucks of America." [135]The Marquis de Chastellux, a French officer, met the Rhode Island regiment in Hartford early in 1781, as they were crossing Connecticut to their winter quarters in New York State. He noted that they "were Black, strong, robust men." The reason for the separation of the troops may also have had something to do with Friedrich von Schiller's (1759 -1805) release of "The Robbers" that year.

[132] Calkins Carroll. Etal, The Story of America, Readers Ass. Inc Pleasantville NY Digest 1975 p.48

[133] The Columbia Encyclopedia. Columbia University Press. 3rd Edition 1963 p907

[134] The Negro in the American Revolution chapel hill Benjamin Quarles, pg.198 (from Connecticut Black Soldiers 1775-1783 by David White 1973. Pequot Press Chester Connecticut. Pg 32)

[135] Travels in North America in the years 1780-82, Marquis de Chastellux Howard Rice pg229 (Chapel Hill 1963)(from Connecticut Black Soldiers 1775-1783 by David White 1973. Pequot Press Chester Connecticut.pg 33)

Before this era theologians like Jacobus Elisa Johannes Capitein a Dutch Christian minister, tried to find ways to preach a doctrine which would pacify the large population and justified extreme measures including slavery, but there were too many people. Writers expressed this emerging enlightenment, which brought on a renewed sense of contempt for the wealthy Moors. And the revolutionary fever spread throughout Europe and America.

Figure 46 Jacobus Elisa Johannes Capitein 1717-1747

Shiller's work is significant, because he is one of only, [136]"one hundred and seventy authors, who wrote during the entire century from 1740-1840, of a population of over forty million people in the Prussian region. In Shiller's story the protagonist, [137]"Karl Van Moor in his eagerness to reach the goal (of wading off the vandals), thinks to penetrate them not by skill and patience, but by open force. Injury and disappointment exasperate rather than instruct him. His expected heroes, turn out to be average men and his friends, smiling traitors, who lead him to destruction. The intensity of his suffering has made him still further incapable of reflection. Stung by fury into blind action he looks upon the world, a den of thieves. "He went empty away in purse and hope... Encircled by murderers and serpents hissing around, he is destined to dwell in eternal night." Within a few weeks on March 8th, 1782, ninety-six members of the Moravian church in Pennsylvania, were massacred, and this was just the beginning of a type of home grown terrorism. Schiller's message herald a setting sun for these children of the sun, and came at a time when [138]"Barbarian hordes of great migration through Europe, had succumbed to the infection of the civilized settled communities." This wave of Aryan immigrants everywhere, prompted Thomas Malthus' suggestions on reducing this quickly expanding population. The problem was keeping the overwhelming size of the population in check, in an era where the mass-produced revolver was not yet invented. Men still fought with iron vests and swords, in open combat, so the large population easily over run the army. Everyone could see the writing on the wall. Benjamin Franklin correctly predicted, that [139]"the conquerors would engross as many offices and exact as many tributes on the labor of the conquered to maintain their new offices. Then they would discourage their marriages to diminish them, while the Saxons increased on their abandoned lands."

Schiller more like a prophet than a writer of fiction, was predicting the fall of the Moors from all Europe. His Fiesco's Conspiracy at Genoa provided the political slogan, [140]"the Moor had done his job; the Moor can go," a revolutionary chant, which thanked the Moors for building their country by expelling them. The atmosphere, after Schiller's call to arms, was one which led to centuries of still ongoing warfare, from the French revolution, to World War II, nearly two hundred years later. The growing mistrust is the reason why the Black Ops were sent on the most sensitive missions. This also prompted the separation of congregations. The African Methodist Episcopal among the first newly segregated congregations, was established in Pennsylvania in 1792.

---

[136] Outlines of German Literature Joseph Gostwick & Robert Harrison Holt & Williams F. W Christern 1873 p. 4

[137] The life of Friedrich Schiller comprehending an examination of his works. Thomas Carlyle, Dana Estes and Co. Boston 1825 (4-5)

[138] Lafayette a life 1936 by Andreas latzko translated from German by E. W. Dickens 79

[139] The founding Fathers, Benjamin Franklin in His Own Words. Thomas Fleming Newsweek NY 1972 p102

[140] Schiller, Friedrich. Fiesco or, The Genoese Conspiracy, A Tragedy.

Figure 47 Absalom Jones, African Episcopal of ST. Thomas and Richard Allen, African Methodist Episcopal 1792

Hanson prepared the nation for war, by appointing George Washington as General of the Army. Lafayette tried to swing Washington, but Washington preached neutrality. He saw an opportunity for America to be a nation like none other, to "cultivate peace and harmony with all," and warned that they should "guard against the imposters of pretended patriotism." Washington's diplomatic philosophy prevailed. At the end of the war in 1783, the Americans were victorious. The British soldiers fled and Jefferson and Lafayette followed. When Jefferson entered Britain, he complained that, "the villages announce a general poverty, as did the labor of women, which he considered "a sign of a backward society." [141]"The Bretons proud and defiant… were known in France as the most recalcitrant of the country's subjects and the best possible instructors for acquainting Lafayette with the abuses. Upon his return to France, he was haunted by the abuse of the aristocracy, and less capable of hiding his contempt. A courtier asked "what are a few thousand francs more or less to the king," and Lafayette replied, "the sweat of a whole village."

While in France, they met with the French committee of revolutionary instigators, who were trying to illuminate the French people. This time there was a greater need for deliberation. The Spanish empire collapsed after the expulsion of the Moors and the British, were forced to bring the monarchy back to avert complete collapse. Thus, the new generation of revolutionaries, needed to be more calculating. It was not enough, like "robbers," to merely rob the rich and confiscate their property, they needed to follow the trail of the merchants to take over the markets and set up new ones in their place. Lafayette started plotting a revolution, that would not only dethrone the nobles, but sustain the country after they were deposed. He [142]"addressed the French committee on American tobacco with strategies to end the tobacco monopoly, and on May 30th, 1786, "a message came from Vergennes that the Morris monopoly could be broken." The Morris' family of Morrisania, were among the wealthiest families in America. The Morrisania estate, in Westchester County (possibly present-day Bronx Zoo) was owned by this family since the first settlements in the 1600s. Robert Morris,[143]"called the financier of the Revolution" because he was one of the sponsors to have nearly [144]"impoverished himself that he might furnish means to the patriot army." At the end of 1786 Lafayette [145]proposed to the Ambassador of Russia and Portugal a concert of powers against the Barbary States, (Morocco, Algeria, Libya and Tunisia) which were major strongholds of the Ottoman Empire. While they were busy trying to undermine the French government, the American delegates from twelve of the thirteen states gathered in 1787, to draft a general Constitution for the United States of America. At this time the French monarchy, sent soldiers to aid the Americans in their fight against the British. While the French army was away, the gospel of a New World Order spread through France.

[141]Lafayette a life 1936 by Andreas latzko translated from German by E. W. Dickens p. 115

[142]Letters of Thomas Jefferson retrieved from: Thomas Jefferson, A Strange Case of Mistaken Identity by Alf J Mapp Jr. Madison Books 1987

[143] Know the Signers of the Declaration of Independence by, George Ross 1963 US

[144] The Youth's History of the United States Vol I by, Edward. Ellis A.M New York 1887 pg. 179

[145] Ibid: pg255

Taking France

Figure 48 a) William Ansah Sessarakoo, June 1750. by Gabriel Mathias (d. 1804) British Museum. see ZBA2711. b) King Louis XVI 1754-1793

The king took advantage of Lafayette's popularity with the masses and his sense of duty and honor to the crown, and made him commander of the army. But [146]"the Turkish despotism of the regime was maddening Lafayette" The two privileged classes, the clergy and the nobility or No ability as the Cromwellians referred to them, owned nine tenths of the land and were free from taxation, and the remaining tenth sustained them. He witnessed the depravity of 30 million people who lived on a fraction of what the aristocracy squandered. [147]"Innumerable beggars covered the country like a swarm of locust, and the state was compelled to organize a sort of barrack system for them: anyone found to be wandering without means of subsistence was required to be lodged at once in the nearest institution. And the institutions were always filled to overflowing, with hundreds squeezed together sick and healthy alike. Inmates were dying like flies every night and yet for every vacant place there were two waiting at the door to receive a plateful of watery soup."

Lafayette decided that he could only undermine the French regime from within, by creating the citizen guards the "Garde Nationale de Paris." These men who were ridiculed as "SansChollotes," because they fought without pants, were turned into soldiers. "To recognize the new national Guards, Lafayette added the white between the red and blue colors of the flag." His mission was clear, "I bring you here a new cockade, which will go round the world as a symbol of an institution, both civic and military, which must triumph over antiquated tactics of Europe, because it will leave the autocrat governments only the choice between being beaten by eternal powers if they do not imitate it, or overthrown if they do." "Like a giant unchained, the whole nation of thirty millions summoned up its limbs by a single wrench from the rusted chains of the past. The French people of 1789 unable to read, now saw the rays of light penetrating the walls that once obscured their enlightenment. They could no longer be put-off by the church's reminder of the life to come. Once this enlightenment came, it could not

Figure 49 a) Copper coin of Barbados 1792 b) Last Guinean coin of king George

be suppressed."The mob was now christened "the nation" by "high treason." In October of 1789 women gathered on the streets marching with the cry "du pain, du pain," incessantly calling for bread," by November, Jefferson and Lafayette gave birth to the French Revolution. The Royal **Vendee** revolted against the "national" reforms, but in 1797 the first copper pennies were minted in England and by 1813 the British were weaned off of Guinean gold.

---

[146] Lafayette a life 1936 by Andreas latzko translated from German by E. W. Dickens 133-136, 143-155,159, 164
[147] Ibid:

Figure 50 General Alexandre Dumas (1762-1806) by Olivier Pichat (1825-1912) - Musée Alexandre Dumas

Once the ruling powers were killed off, the only contenders to fill the vacuum were Lafayette and Napoleon. But Lafayette declined the opportunity to seize power. Napoleon Bonaparte has been credited with the mastery of the French revolution, but that distinct honor belonged to Lafayette, who was considered a [148]"Cromwell." It is through a closer examination of Lafayette, that the general organization and pattern of the revolutions becomes clear. Dumas who was a general in the French army, was referred to by the German soldiers as *"the Black devil,"* he relates that Napoleon secured victory with a handshake, at a time when he should have killed him. After Robespierre, the executioner died, [149]"the egalite were being released from prison… including the pretty creole Josephine, Napoleon's ex-wife." Morris arrived in Vienna in 1796 to ransom Marie Antoinette's daughter the only survivor of the royal family. The poor emigres who not long ago received him in their luxurious homes in Paris… marshals, ministers, dukes, and counts who owed their fortunes to the empire, were running to and fro like ants whose heap had been disturbed. Many from this disturbed heap of Creoles, fled France in 1797 on the Frigate Creole and settled on creole islands like Dominca St.Lucia and in America.

Nostradamus a Jewish Seer from France predicted this period of role reversal, in the 16th century. *We will see a great people tormented, and the holy law in utter ruin. Christendom under other laws, when a new source of gold and silver is found. Two revolutions will be caused by the evil Scyth-bearer. Who will make a change of Kingdoms and Centuries. Nostradamus (1503–1566)*

Atheism replaced Christianity while the English and French revolutions instigated by the Scyths or Aryans, changed the Kingdoms and centuries of history; with changes to the seats of power. Then this was solidified in 1844 by the discovery of gold in America; which gave the new government a new source of revenue.

Figure 51 a) 19th century image of king toffa of the kingdom of Dahomey from Malerische Studien, Neuchatel b)Le serment_des_Ancêtres The Oath of the Ancestors, by Guillaume Guillon Lethière. 1821 This captures the soul of the 19th century and volatile transition of power.

---

[148] Lafayette a life 1936 by Andreas latzko translated from German by E. W. Dickens266
[149] IBID

Taking America

After Jefferson returned to the US, inspired by the successful overthrow of the French monarchy, an influx of French rebels came with him. He arrived to find, that a new constitution established a government of three equal branches that could not simply be dissolved by deposing its head. The new government was vastly expanded in power with many surrogates of delegated authority. The ranks of which seemed closed to Jefferson, [150]he was shocked to hear of the constitutional convention's rule to secrecy, and considered this secrecy so abominable a precedent. He was so infuriated by the union of the independent states; that in a letter to Elbridge Gerry, (one of only twelve of the signers who survived to the end of his presidency, and who the term Gerrymandering was named for) Jefferson stated, "I am for preserving to the states, the powers not yielded them by the union... I am not for transferring all the powers of the states to the General government, and all those of that government to the executive."

Emboldened by the success in France and his own army of French revolutionaries, Jefferson established a new party, the Democratic Party, to run against, the Federalist, or Whig party, which accused him of being a Jacobin (an instigator of the French Revolution). In 1791 congress devised a strategy to help men like Morris recoup their losses. They created the First National Bank in America and elected Alexander Hamilton as the first secretary of the treasury. In July of that year, Jefferson wrote to T. Paine (another one to survive to the end of his presidency) to say these timid men, were "a sect high in name but small in number," In fact, the old oligarchy had been dwindling to just a few survivors and could now, easily be deposed; and Jefferson confessed to being [151E]"a hypochondriac Englishman about to write with a pistol the last chapter of history."

Adams defeated Jefferson in 1796 and with an increasing body of illegitimate politicians, he was the last president to address joint sessions of congress until Woodrow Wilson, more than a century later. Adams took steps to diminish Jefferson's increasing power and passed the Alien Sedition Act to deport the foreigners and make it harder for the new French immigrants to vote. The secret was out, in April 1796 Jefferson exposed his secret enemies. "Against us are all the officers of the government, all who *want to be officers*, all timid men who prefer the calm of despotism to the boisterous sea of liberty..." the His writings reveal. Cromwellian views about the mental inferiority of Blacks. A charge which Benjamin Banneker vigorously challenged. Benjamin F. noted that the Jeffersonians had the remarkable skill of "destroying governments," but had yet to prove that they could actually govern, because at this point the only models were "seeds of their dissolution."

The new American government now needed separate territory for their headquarters and Benjamin Banker, in the tradition of African civil engineers, [152]"produced a plan so grand that it provided for the traffic of London and elegance of Versailles. The conception proved that the US understood the vastness of their task. The traveler who visited

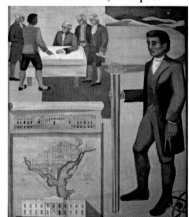

Figure 52 "Benjamin Banneker: Surveyor-Inventor-Astronomer," by M. Seelbinder, Recorder of Deeds building Washington, D.C. photo by Highsmith, C. 1946-, LOC.GOV

[150] Alistair Cooke's America, Alfred A knopf INc, New York 1973 Borzoi Books p153
[151] Thomas Jefferson an intimate history by Fawn H Brodie 1974 pg E (253) F
[152] The United States in 1800 by Henry Adams, Man and Society Vol. 6 Gateway to great Books 1963 pg. 322-359

Washington in 1800 got the impression that once completed it would become the object of jealousy and fear." Jefferson run for office again in 1800, and records indicate there was a tie, that Alexander Hamilton an immigrant from the island of Nevis in the Caribbean, Jefferson's arch rival, and a dedicated federalist, casted the tie breaking vote in Jefferson's favor, against another democrat Aaron Burr and Burr later killed Him. Jeremiah Hamilton (1802-1875) a wealthy New York banker also from the West Indies may have been Hamilton's relative.

Jefferson's regime inherited a well-planned democracy that many believed him incapable of maintaining. Upon his appointment for the presidency, New England papers began to campaign against him. [153]The New England Palladium warned "Our churches will be prostrated". The Connecticut Courant warned, "there is scarcely a possibility that we shall escape civil war... Murder, robbery, rape, adultery, and incest will be openly taught and practiced." Every prediction of the New England papers would soon prove true. The nation quickly began to disintegrate into civil war. The war was more secret than civil, Jefferson's enemies had no idea of the master plans, and while many believed he hated Blacks and he said as much, he had an entire family of Black people who made that idea sound preposterous.

Jefferson's enemies were a secret that only his allies were aware of and they picked them off one by one. By the end of his presidency, forty-eight of the fifty-six men, who signed the declaration of independence and comprised the infant government were dead. It was now essentially a new government. But he could not complete his version of American history just yet; because he was [F154]"haunted nightly by the form of Hanson." Hanson appears to have escaped Jefferson's pistol and the fate of the other members of the original government, who died before Jefferson's election, or during his tenure. He out lived Jefferson; so the details of the discussion of the original government and [155]"just what was said and done in this secret conclave was not revealed until fifty years had passed, and the aged James Madison, the last survivor of those who sat there, had been gathered to his fathers." Hanson's name does not appear on the declaration of Independence; but the Declaration of Independence had been kept rolled up and there had been some smudging of the signatures, in the process of rolling and unrolling. In 1877 it was removed from public view and locked in a safe... and then it was finally brought back to Washington in 1944 during WWII nearly two hundred years later.

Burr became a wealthy man, when he married his mistress after her husband's sudden death. In 1798, Morris disappeared after arriving in France to ransom, for the remnant of the French aristocracy. Morris died in May of 1806 and the wealthy estate of the Morris family in Morrisania New York, was then seized, plundered and burned; so with Hamilton dead and the two principle agents of the American banking system officially deposed, this ended the Morris monopoly. [156]George Wythe, one of the original signers of the declaration, was poisoned along with his wife and their son in June 1806. Before his death, Wythe implicated George Sweeny, and although his wife survived, she was barred from testifying, because it was now against Virginia law for a Black person to testify against a White person, so Sweeney was exonerated. Then in July, James Smith died, and all of his personal records were destroyed in a fire.

Napoleon then scoured the world after the fleeing émigrés. His armies were decimated by hunger in Egypt, and completely defeated by Haitians. The

Figure 53 a) Haitian Flag the original flag of France b) the new revolutionary Flag of France.

[153] American Heritage book of Presidents and famous Americans by AH Publishing Co. 1967 pg103 & notes H-J
154 Thomas Jefferson an intimate history by Fawn H Brodie 1974 pg391
[155] The Workers in American History: by James Oneal, National Rip-Saw 1912 pg177
[156]Thomas Jefferson an intimate history by Fawn H Brodie 1974 pg391

Haitian people continue to fly their "deux coloeurs" which only recognized those of *blue blood,* (the aristocrats) and the colored or mixed-race people. Napoleon's failed quests to conquer all of Ottoman territory, led New France on the verge of bankruptcy. The new American government in need of a strong ally, helped to finance Napoleon's Wars, with a grant of 16 million dollars in 1803, under the guise of a Louisiana purchase and without any approval from congress. A tremendous sum, not only considering that Napoleon had considered this territory "lost," but also because at this time, [157]"the nominal capital of all the banks, including the First bank of the United States, fell short of 29,000,000." Jefferson handed more than half of all the money in the treasury to Napoleon, for territory, that he had no power to defend. At a time when the people of [158]New Orleans built the first high powered light draft steam boat which solved the problem of navigating the powerful down stream currents of the Mississippi river," and were well on their way to secure ports to the Mid-West.

Figure 54 Members of the Louisiana convention & Assembly 1868

Louisiana

[159]"Louisiana, was a Creole state,'[160]of roughly a quarter of a million Creoles… not subject to Napoleonic forces; but "as the number of Anglo-Saxons about them multiplied, the Creoles became more aggressively conscious of their language and culture, and more determined to preserve them."[161]Nowhere in America was there a Black planter aristocracy comparable with that of Louisiana… wealthy families and successful business men, were involved in nearly all phases of economic activity. James Derham 1758-180? was possibly the first doctor in the state. Men like Norbert Rillieux, patented a sugar refining process in 1846.[162] Cyprian Richard owned one of the largest plantations which employed almost a hundred slaves… Pierre Cazanave a merchant and commission Broker increased his earning from 100K to a million from 1850 to 1857. Thomy Lafon, was said to be worth half a million dollars at his death, and by the outbreak of civil war, men of color owned more than 15,000,000 worth of property." This prosperity came to an end after the massacre of 1887, over 300 intellectuals were killed, and the tactics of intimidation, murder and fraud left White supremacists in control of the government to this day.

Ohio

When Ohio became a state in 1803, many Blacks were established there. Henry Boyd Kentucky 1802-1886 was one of the most successful furniture makers. Samuel Wilcox 1846-1903 a free mason was the first and most successful grocer in Cincinnati. His business was extended to Boston New York and Baltimore. Robert Gordon moved from Virginia to Cincinnati, with 15,000 in 1847 to become one of the

[157] The United States in 1800 by Henry Adams, Man and Society Vol. 6 Gateway to great Books 1963 pg.

[158] Alistair Cooke's America, Alfred A knopf INc, New York 1973 Borzoi Books p 193

[159] Histoire des États-Unis, C.F. Chamerot, 1894 pg. 124

[160] Spiller, Robert etal Literary History of the United States, 3rd ED 1963 pg. 684

[161] A different Vision of African American Economic Thought. Thomas D Boston Psychology Press 1997. p186

[162] A Pictorial History of Black Americans, 5th revised edition by Langston Hughes, Milton Meltzer, and C. Eric Lincoln. Crown Publishers New York 1983 p

most successful coal miners there and the C. F. Patterson family, were established auto manufacturers.

In 1807 after Jefferson paid a huge sum to Napoleon, he placed an embargo on American merchants, the most influential and powerful political forces, which he depended on for tariffs from trade. This strategy meant to cripple the North Africans, but also the American merchants that were allied to them. As president, [163]Jefferson was still restricted by a legislative framework which was acting on behalf of a people who were more sophisticated in self-government. The new rulers still lacked access to many of the natural resources, or naval and global dominance, which could guarantee their supremacy. They were still forced to play by the rules of the old-world powers, who controlled the most important maritime passages. The Trans-Atlantic Slave trade was mostly a trade of soldiers, but more specifically the detaining of Caucasian, American and European soldiers, by the Ottoman forces; because the Mediterranean waters, were heavily guarded. (**Notice the comparative value of the Guinea.**)

> The late peace of Spain with Algiers is said to have cost from three to five millions of dollars. Having received the money, they take the vessels of that nation on the most groundless pretexts ; counting, that the same force which bound Spain to so hard a treaty, may break it with impunity.
>
> Their treaty with France, which had expired, was about two years ago renewed for fifty years. The sum given at the time of renewal is not known. But presents are to be repeated every ten years, and a tribute of one hundred thousand dollars to be annually paid. Yet perceiving that France, embarrassed at home with her domestic affairs, was less capable of acting abroad, they took six vessels of that nation in the course of the last year, and retain the captives, forty-four in number, in slavery.
>
> It is the opinion of Captain O'Brien, that those nations are best treated who pay a smaller sum in the beginning, and an annual tribute afterwards. In this way he informs us that the Dutch, Danes, Swedes, and Venetians pay to Algiers, from twenty-four to thirty thousand dollars a year, each ; the two first in naval stores, the two last chiefly in money. It is supposed, that the peace of the Barbary States costs Great Britain about sixty thousand guineas, or two hundred and eighty thousand dollars a year. But it must be noted that these facts cannot be authentically advanced ; as from a principle of self-condemnation, the governments keep them from from the public eye as much as possible.
>
> Nor must we omit finally to recollect, that the Algerines, attentive to reserve always a sufficient aliment for their piracies, will never extend their peace beyond certain limits, and consequently, that we may find ourselves in the case of those nations to whom they refuse peace at any price.

[164]   **OFFICIAL PAPERS.**   **525**

Meanwhile Napoleon now backed by financial support, charged through Europe. [165]"When war broke out between France and Austria in 1809, Frederick William formed a corps of "Black Brunswickers," and captured Brunswick. Austria, a land of diverse peoples, was then ruled by the Magyar minority. The conflicting nationalistic aspirations of this diverse population set the revolutionary

---

[163] Ibid.124

[164] American State papers, Documents, Legislative and Executive of the Congress of the United States. (pg. 105 The Mediterranean Wars) from

[165] The Columbia Encyclopedia. Columbia University Press. 3rd Edition 1963 p764, 136-137.

movements of this age against each other. This division sharpened the opposition but maintained the autocracy there for another century. These nations were forced to sign inequitable treaties, to maintain the vital trading relationships or risk economic depression. Jefferson's successor, James Madison (1809-1817) had served as Jefferson's Secretary of State and opposed Hamilton's proposals for handling government finances, because "he felt it unduly bestowed wealth and power upon Northern financiers." He allowed for the collapse of the first National Bank in 1811, and the country entered a deep recession.

As the New England papers predicted, the years following Jefferson's presidency, were marked by a gradual disintegration into war. The nation lacked a central authority on military action, trade or a common enemy. While Jefferson desired the friendship of France and England against the North Africans, many of the American merchants preferred the inverse. [166]From 1812-1814, the Battle of Baltimore also called the Hanson riots, was caused by an attack on the Federalist newspaper office. The original State house now called the White House, was burned along with the Capitol, the Library of Congress, along with all of the records and the navy yard, which housed the American warships. The Ships of wealthy merchants like Paul Cuffe, loaded with cargo were seized and this led to the financial upheaval of many. When the British attacked Baltimore's Fort McHenry, the Americans resisted with

Figure 55 Francis Scott Key. (The hands do not match the face.) Located in the National Museum of American History

great courage. Once the fog of the smoke was cleared up, by the Dawn's early light, Francis Scott Key saw that the American flag was still there. His emotional reaction became the lyrics for "The Star-Spangled Banner,"

And where are the foes who so vauntingly swore. That the havoc of war, and the battle's confusion, A home and a country should leave us no more: Their blood has washed out their foul footsteps' pollution; No refuge could save the hireling and slave from the terror of flight, or gloom of the grave; but the star-Spangled Banner in triumph yet waves O'er the land of the Free and the home of the brave. The *hireling and slave* were the British commoners now soldiers who successfully defeated the Moors and emancipated themselves, "Never to be slaves again."

American writer F. Scott Fitzgerald (1896-1941) was named for Francis Scott Key, a distant cousin of his paternal grandmother. He described himself as [167]half Black Irish and half old American stock with the usual exaggerated ancestral pretensions. [168]"He had early developed an inferiority complex in the midst of a family where the Black Irish half had the money and looked down upon the poor Maryland side of the family. Key's Black Iris roots are especially significant in analyzing the identity of those invading, versus those defending. The invaders had succeeded in chasing them from Spain, England and France. America was the final frontier, there was no place left to run. The invaders were on their way *"A home and country to leave us no more:"*

Although the war resulted in the restoration of the State to the Federalist Party, the Democrats had a far greater agenda up their sleeves, one which required the rewriting of the story. In 1815 Congress unsuspectingly approved the purchase of Thomas Jefferson's library, to replace the one destroyed in the

---

[166] Histoire des États-Unis by Grégoire Jeanne C.F. Chamerot, 1894 pg. 402

[167] The Letters of F. Scott Fitzgerald (New York Charles Scribner's Sons, 1963) accessed from Le Vot, Andre F. Scott Fitzgerald a Biography 1983 pg 7

[168] Shain, Charles F. Scott Fitzgerald

fire. A new government and new citizens would soon replace the old and with this transition came a brand-new story and history. But even with political control, there was still the issue of economic and military dominion. The markets of the West Indies and other areas of the New World were controlled by the same Old-World powers. Their economic survival depended not only on new treaties, but on maintaining the ones already in place. Madison was forced to open the Second Bank of America in 1816.

Jefferson was also aware of the influence which knowledge and education had on society. It was not enough to uplift the whites, he had to cripple the Blacks. Thus, he was actively involved in rewriting and revising the historic perspective to set the stage for taking complete control of the global lens. For the French who succeeded in ejecting their monarchy, a complete revision was simple. [169]"He collaborated in revised editions of French historians Francois Soules', Histoire des troubles de'l Amerique et Anglaise and Jean Nicolas Demeunier's great Encyclopedia Methodique; but he warned the German, not to trust two of his Northern contributors, Jedidiah Morse and Noah Webster…"

Noah Webster, was among New England writers, who fought against the gild. These writers refused the veneering of this era and urged their countrymen to remember their origin. Jefferson must have despised this unrelenting authenticity, which threatened to keep alive the very information which he was trying to erase. Jefferson was not naïve, he was well aware that the upliftment of his people was a great challenge. He commented while on his trip in Europe, [170]"I am filled with alarms for the event of eruptions making on us by the Goths, Ostrogoth's, Visigoths and Vandals, lest they should reconquer us to our original barbarianism." Despite the challenge, Jefferson believed that what would improve the social standing of his countrymen, was enlightenment through new education and alternative facts.

Jefferson thought that they could learn from the examples of Spain and deport the Blacks, in this way they would be deleted from American history; but fear of a collapse of the economy prevented him from trying it out. He decided instead, to open the flood gates, so Whites could come in and gradually assume the positions of the Blacks. Benjamin Franklin lamented that this the influx of Germanic Europeans, would likely 'Germanize' America, more than Americanize the Germans. The other issue was that the President was chosen by the electoral college, so many Blacks were transplanted into new regions to establish the 30,000 required to appoint state and federal representatives. During this period, Harriet

Figure 56 Immigrants arriving at Ellis Island NY 1906 LOC.gov

Tubman (1819-1913) was actively recruiting Blacks from the South where Blacks outnumbered Whites two to three, to counter the influx of new White immigrants to New England. This mass transplantation of people fueled the need for ground transportation which led to the development of the first railroad system. Burr with the aid of Zebulon Pike, worked at bringing in German immigrants and [171]the McManus clan had devised a scheme to settle German immigrants in Texas. The race was on.

---

[169] Thomas Jefferson, A Strange Case of Mistaken Identity by Alf J Mapp Jr. Madison Books 1987 pg. 232
[170] Letters of Thomas Jefferson, A Strange Case of Mistaken Identity by Alf J Mapp Jr. Madison Books 1987. (notes 5,6) 253
[171] Fallen founder, the life of Aaron Burr Viking Nancy Isenberg 402

Webster, Stowe among many other prolific writers of the time, continued to teach the old history. Although Webster and Stowe were both legendary figures, and still have museums of their homes in Connecticut, I was unable to find their most controversial writings there. Webster assumed that the barbaric history of his people, was due to destitution. He believed that in time and with the understanding of the grace of God, which extended salvation to his people, this nature would be overcome with an understanding of the truth, the "Old Man" could evolve into a new one.

Examine the following excerpt from Webster's text book on ethics. [172]

In the long period which elapsed from the first migration of the Japhetic families into Europe, to the Roman conquests in Gaul and Britain, and for some ages after. the sole business of the people was war and the chase; The young men at eighteen or twenty years of age, took the buckler, the sword and the lance, and were then obliged to seek their subsistence by the chase, or by plundering their neighbors.

It is painful to cast our eyes over Europe, and survey a population of many millions, engaged, for two or three thousand years, in making war on each other. one tribe or nation making inroads on another, slaughtering men, women and children, or expelling them from their residence, and plundering them of all their possessions.

But of the fact, the concurring testimony of authors leaves us no room for doubt. The practice of plundering may have originated in the poverty and distress of nations, who had no other means of procuring subsistence;

Yet the rude nations of Europe had such imperfect notions of right and wrong, that they maintained war to be just, alledging that force constitutes right—that the Deity intended the strong should plunder the weak, who must abandon the goods which they have not power to defend.

Jefferson preferred to ignore or rewrite the past and challenged the legitimacy of the Christian doctrine. He was influenced by Rousseau; who felt that "Laws were instituted merely to consolidate the power of the oppressors over the oppressed." He believed that the laws, ideology and doctrines established in society needed to be challenged. Jefferson now had the power to rewrite the story. This was the objective of Darwin's fine tuning of the ancient barbaric theology of survival of the fittest. In this new story the Germanic people were the creators of democracy and Republican government. Alexander Hanson, protested this change,[173]there is no solid ground to believe that the Saxons differed in their fundamental institutions from their German brethren, or those other hordes of northern barbarians that subjugated civilized Europe…" Others like Samuel Elliot Morison, retained their skepticism believing

---

[172] Letters to a Young Gentleman Commencing His Education: With a Brief History of the United States by Noah Webster Howe & Spalding, S. Converse, printer, 1823 received by Harvard College in 1879. Pg. 125-129

[173] Publications Relative to the Difference of Opinion Between the Governor and the Council [of Maryland] on Their Respective Powers by Alexander Contee Hanson Frederick Green, Printer to the State, 1803 pg.125

that [174]"these children of nature white or red could no more be made to respect a treaty than dogs can be kept from fighting by the friendship of their masters." This experiment in the forces of human nature would soon be tested in the power of "nature vs nurture." The Jeffersonian model simply gave the New Man a new history. One that they could be proud of and transformed by.

Figure 57 Immigrants in English class given by Training Service of the Department of Labor in Ford Motor Co. Factory, Detroit, Michigan

The next president, James Monroe (1817-1825) proposed the famous Monroe Doctrine, which would generate revenue by taking over established territory. This program of territorial usurpation, or colonization required the immigration of Europeans to take over the strategic areas which the new politicians needed to maintain control. Thus [175]in the second and third decades of the nineteenth century, the American government advertised a "promised land," to Europeans and a heavier flow of German immigration set in. By [176]"1870 there was a vast increase in the number of immigrants and in the second and third decades of the nineteenth century a heavier flow of German immigration set in, nearly a million arrived each year." The dramatic increase in whites simply diluted the concentration of Blacks. Then these were given land, citizenship and the right to vote to affect the political makeup of the government. They arrived to claim territory and benefits that those who labored for, were denied. As these new immigrants climbed their way out of American slums and into suburbia, they left behind the Blacks, who remained the perpetual object of scorn and oppression.

At this time, in the struggle for White supremacy and global dominance, the US government passed one legislation after another to cripple the Black economy. White soldiers assumed control of the military, in the form of national guards or police officers, with the right to kill all non-white civilians, a legacy which for some continues to this day. Blacks were also barred from bringing charges or testifying against their injustices. The new immigrants came in without skills, or education, to find an abundance of open fields filled with fruits already planted. Many received free land and laborers to work it, produce food and build their homes. While the new immigrants were given every tool to aid in their development, Blacks were forbidden from reading and new laws were enacted to diminish, and THEN enslave the Black population. Once the Blacks had successfully laid the foundation and built them up, then Jefferson imagined that it would be time for "the day of separation." And when that day came, and 'the Moor had done his job, the Moor must go." Tears filled the trails of those who would be stripped of their possessions, ripped from their homes and many were sent into the first concentration camps.

This strategy for revolution of government were so successful in France, and successfully on its way as planned in America, that Jefferson outlined his vision. He believed that when the day of separation of the races came, they would have [177]"Prussia, Austria and Italy, as they had, already taken England, France and Spain." Jefferson understood that the antiquated weapons of this era were no match to the massive number of Europeans ready to be transplanted into foreign countries. Spies were being

[174] Alistair Cooke's America, Alfred A knopf Inc., New York 1973 Borzoi Books p 161

[175] Spiller, Robert etal Literary History of the United States, 3rd ED 1963 pg. 679.

[176] ibid pg.677

[177] The United States in 1800 by Henry Adams, Man and Society Vol. 6 Gateway to great Books 1963 pg.344

dispatched throughout the world under the guise of Christian missions. Soon the takeover through colonization began. By 1820 there were 80,000 British applicants for land in South Africa and in 1824, Germans begun immigrating to Brazil. Meanwhile every effort was employed to restrict the growth and survival of the native Blacks and to cut them out of society and the global economy.

At this point, the arrangement of facts tells such a dramatically new story, that the reader naturally must question! [178]"What was it that turned the European peasant into a new man within half an hour of landing in New York?" It may be that the [179]"predictions of Schiller demanded fulfillment." The new immigrants came inspired to take America, as their ancestors had taken Rome. [180]A new life was awakening among students and professors in universities, and at Berlin Fitche, which served to kindle a fervor of patriotism. "Germans the voices of your ancestors are sounding from the oldest times-the men who destroyed Rome's despotism, the heroes who gave their lives to preserve these mountains… which you allow a foreign despot to claim. Shall your descendants be tempted into falsehood to hide their disgrace? Must they say No we are not descended from the Germans? You are the descendants of those heroes who triumphed over corrupted Rome." The Germans had been disgraced for centuries, by a history which they now had the power to rewrite. They now had the opportunity to trade place with the powerful.

Suddenly the new immigrants [181]"stood in the world a new order of man without an ounce of superfluous flesh on his nervous supple body. Few human beings, however sluggish, could long resist the temptation to acquire power. Reversing the old-world system, the American stimulant increased in energy as it reached the lowest and most ignorant class, dragging and whirling them upward as in the blast of a furnace. The penniless and homeless Scotch or Irish immigrant was caught and consumed by it; for every stroke of the ax and the hoe made him a capitalist and made gentlemen of his children. Wealth was the strongest agent for moving the mass of mankind; but political power was hardly less tempting to the more intelligent better educated swarms of American born citizens, and the instinct of activity, *once created, seemed heritable and permanent in the race.*"

As the new immigrants assumed the identity of the old Americans, the old grudgingly with much resistance and strife were forced to relinquish and adapt to the new. It was a classic tale of trading places, so that once the roles were reversed the pretenders begun to be molded, into the status of "high birth" and those of high birth were reduced to slaves and paupers or completely erased. This is around the time when the 'Niger' became a contemptuous object of scorn and sarcasm. This was captured in the contemporary stories of Mark Twain (1835-1910). One of Twain's novels, Huckleberry Finn, breaks one of the cardinal rules of the gilded era, which was never to portray Blacks, as powerful. Twain tells the story of a runaway Nigger and a young man who gave the account that he came [182]"across him in the woods and he (the Nigger) said if I hollered he'd cut my livers out-and told me to lay down and stay where I was: and I done it. Been there ever since; afraid to come out." Twain's realism in the portrayal of the still evolving White Americans, their crude language and manners, made his work extremely popular, but was muted in later years. His works, capture the era of transition from his tale of trading places, in "The Prince and the Pauper," to the story of "A Connecticut Yankee in king Arthur's court." The latter is reminiscent of Thomas Jefferson's journey to Europe a few decades earlier. The names were changed, but the essence of the story echoes Jefferson's journey into the old world with the knowledge and perspective of a world

[178] The United States in 1800 by Henry Adams, Man and Society Vol. 6 Gateway to great Books 1963 pg. 320

[179] Outlines of German Literature by Joseph Gostwick & Robert Harrison Holt & Williams F. W. Christern 1873 p.421

[180] Ibid: 421-423

[181] Ibid: pg. 345

[182] Twain, Mark The Favorite Works of Mark Twain Garden City Publishing Co. INC 1939 p591

which seemed not just a few hours, but centuries ahead in time. In the thirteenth chapter, Twain describes the system of injustice experienced by the White subjects in Europe, who represented over seventy percent of the population. A system which experienced a change only in face a few years later, when Jack London visited London. The undertones of Twain's writings, lament the transition which was taking shape. [183]In "The Devil's Race Track," Twain saw history as a treadmill of endlessly and monotonously repeated events. And he conceives of a universal food chain... of devourers who in their turn become victims, humankind and God included." This view sheds light on his fear that these paupers who were now to become "the nation," were acting now like Devil's. Whereas they rightfully wrested themselves from tyranny, within fifty years, the new rulers had surpassed their former tyrants' cruelty.

*Figure 58 **a)** Jacques Louis David, Paris 1799 **b)** Congress of Paris 1851*

Asenath Nicholson, visited Europe during this era and described the site of the anciene class reduced to famine in 1844 after their soil was probably poisoned. [184]"Come proud boasting man; come, high-born and titled lady, look at your portrait. Here are men, one year ago, with robust look and manly step, standing erect in the face of high heaven... where is boasting then? It is excluded. On what a slender thread hangs all of our standing here! The blasting of one root... amid fields of plenty and gardens of beauty, prostrates in a few short weeks so many of the robust and blooming, and makes them an abhorring to all flesh, a prey to dogs and rats almost before the breath had departed. Never among the halls of the great have I since seen the rich, the gay, and the honored, laughing in the sunshine of pride and vanity, but my thoughts turned to the sickening sight of that night of the famine."

*Figure 59 **a)** Burning of Will Brown Omaha Nebraska 1919 **b)** Lynching of Thomas Skipp and Abraham Smith Indiana 1930. The story of Black American genocide is a lot greater than the few instances of lynchings. Notice the attire of the vilans, they don't appear to be poor wretches, these were probably police officers, educators, clergy and other respectable members of society.*

---

[183] Tuckey, John and Watson, Richard: The Devil's Race Track: Mark Twain's Great Dark Writings: the best From which was the Dream and the Fables of Man...University of California Press, 1980

[184] Loose papers: or facts gathered during eight years residence in Ireland, Scotland, England, France and Germany. Nicholson, Asenath 1853

State by State Destruction of the World's Top Five Percent

Figure 60 Wealthy American sailor c.1780 (Newport Historical Society).

[185]On December 20, 1790 Samuel Slater, built the first American Cotton mill in Pawtucket, Rhode Island, for this he was considered the father of the industrial revolution and in 1803, roughly 20,000 Negroes were transported by New England traders to Georgia and South Carolina. But by 1808, Jefferson banned the immigration of Blacks to force, New England manufacturers to hire new White immigrants. Despite Jefferson's prohibition on Black immigration, Northern States began more aggressive recruitment of Black soldiers, to initiate civil war. At this time English and Saxson-American spies were dispatched into Africa, to stop the incessant arrival of Africans from the source, and they operated as missionaries on anti-slavery campaigns.

In 1823 when the first British spies, Denham, Clapperton, and Oudney arrived in Bornu, they travelled from Mourzuk to Kouka and found [186]"a cavalry drawn up in line and extending right and left, quite as far as (he) could see. The Bornu troops remained quite steady without noise or confusion. Their horses were also defended by plates of iron, brass silver, just leaving sufficient room for the eyes." (These soldiers and their performance and presence, akin to the American musical tradition of *Stomping* were)[187]"Arrayed in armor like medieval European Knights, the cavalry men terrorized the central Sudan for more than 200 years, attacking in close formation to the shrill sound of long war trumpets... These Negro knights, according to the British report, "were habited in coats of nail composed of iron chain, which covered them from the throat to the knees, and their richly caparisoned horses moved with great precision and expertness through intricate maneuvers. Even the greeting given to the British combined a strange kind of knightly courtesy with defiant pride. The horsemen rushed at them again and again in a series of mock charges, shouting "welcome" a gesture, which gave the compliment of a declaration of contempt for [our] weakness."

Figure 61 Bornu Soldier from Dixon's diary

---

[185] http://www.americaslibrary.gov/jb/nation/jb_nation_cotton_4.html

[186] Narrative of Travels and Discoveries in Northern and Central Africa, in the Years 1822,1823, and 1824, by Major Denham, Captain Clapperton, and the Late Doctor Oudney, Published by Authority of the Right Honorable Earl Bathurst ... by Major Dixon Denham ... and Captain Hugh Clapperton, of the Royal Navy. Knight as depicted by Dixon.

[187] Davidson, Basil: African Kingdoms, Time Life Books Collection (The Great Ages of Man.) 1978 pg. 30

Robert Brown arrived in Gabon in1844 less than fifty years after some of the exiles of the French Revolution arrived there and almost forty years before the scramble for Africa, and noted that the [188] "traders in Gabon claimed French nationality, inspite of extremely swarthy complexion, which pointed more he thought to a relationship rather near to the natives." Africans dominated the continent, and sent envoys around the world. Their decendants were the French, the Potuguese, the Spainish, the English, the Moors or Boers and other groups that had long commerce with Europe. In 1787, Count Constantine de Volney -- a French historian and politician attributed the French language to the infiltration of Blacks. [189] "Just think, that this race of Black men, today our slave and the object of our scorn, is <u>the very race to which we owe our arts, sciences, and even the use of speech</u>."

Before this period, the gold mines of Timbuktu remained heavily guraded and the continent heavily fortified. These people don't speak french, English or Portuguees because it was brought to Africa, but the contrary. Language can only be transferred through intimate connection, this is why Latin died out throughout Europe along with its native Latin speakers, despite its long extensive history there. Blacks were barred from reading and general education, and if whites considered them too inferior to converse with them, there would be no way for such a mass language transfer. The so called pidgin languages of West Africa and the Gala of Saint Helena provide evidence of the early form of English, as Creole is to French. These remained intact because they developed apart from new standardizations.

*Figure 62 **a)** Elias Boudin **b)** James Forteen 1766-1842 Wealthy Sailmaker. Historical Society of Pennsylvania*

Pennsylvania

From 1830, Johnson forced thousands of people from one of the most established regions in Pennsylvania, and the entire country, to Oklahoma, and new immigrants came in to take their place. He then refused the renewal of the Bank's charter in 1834. The homes of those who refused to move were burned, along with their bank and the African Presbyterian Church. Jackson's successor apposed depositing of government funds into the Bank, which he considered a [190]"government sponsored monopoly;" so by 1837 the Second Bank of America collapsed after the disenfranchised, began to take their money out. For about five years the United States was wracked by the worst depression in its history. The news circulated around the country causing a major uproar. To curtail the spread of information newspaper offices were under attack. The Post Office in Charleston with its delivery of newspapers, was burned in 1835; so the US Postal Service banned the delivery of these materials. There has been a misconception that the territory taken over by the Whites, was empty green pasture. According to Elias Boudin, [191]at this time, there are 22,000 cattle; 7,600 Horses; 46,000 swine; 2,500 sheep; 762 looms; 2488 spinning wheels; 172 wagons; 2,943 ploughs; 10 saw-mills; 31 grist-mills; 62 Blacksmith-shops; 8 cotton machines; 18 schools 18 ferries; and a number of public roads... On the public roads, there are many decent Inns, and houses... The Whites who were coming to replace these people were the epitome of the 'poor, tired and weak.' Many were actually lawless,

---

[188] The Story of Africa and its Explorers, Robert Brown 1896 pg 47

[189] Travels in Syria and Egypt, During the Years 1783, 1784, & 1785, Volume 1 Constantin-François Volney R. Morison, 1801 p. 55. NOW by Joel A. Freeman, Ph.D.

[190] The Presidents of the United States, White House Historical Association: Freidel, Franklin

[191] An Address to The Whites Speech Delivered in the First Presbyterian Church Philadelphia, MAY 26, 1826 by Elias Boudinot, Excerpted by the National Humanities Center for use in a Professional Development Seminar

unskilled criminals, who terrorized Europe and were eager to escape [192]"instances of steady systematic cruelty, in the treatment of their children, which went far beyond anything recorded of slave drivers in (America)." By 1845 Samuel Colt's invention of the mass-produced revolver, promised to revolutionize the war, it was a game changer. The Amistad arrived in Connecticut in 1848, filled with Africans.

Figure 63 Captain of the North Star invited the Moors of North Africa to inspect his new ship.

Around 1850 the North Star yacht surveilled the Mediterranean. The population from Gibraltar to Florence, [193]was a "place of trade and commerce, for here the Turks, Moors, Armenians, Chinese, and Dutch sailors were smoking as if as much at home as in Amsterdam. *In Gibraltar, the sailors encountered a charming merchant named Charley.*

" CHARLEY," THE MOOR.   299

In our shopping expeditions we found ourselves in a curiosity store, kept by a Moor, who is known as " Charley." He is the handsomest blackman I ever saw. His eyes are wondrously fine, but his face has been tattooed in his early youth, when he was a slave in Barbary. Charley has been to Timbuctoo, has been a great traveller, speaks several languages, and has man-aged to accumulate some considerable cash. This man is, in my estimation, " the character " of the town. His costume is throughly Turkish, or, more correctly, Moorish; parts of his dress very costly. In his shop we made many a pleasant lounge, and ate his dates, which

he always brought out. I think that our acquaintance was mutually agreeable ; for certainly Charley, having found favor with our ladies, made extensive sales to all our party, and I fancy at leaving he must have had possession of several hundreds of dollars. His card of business is as follows :

HAGGE SAID GUESUS,
DEALER IN
MOORISH CURIOSITIES, ETC. ETC. ETC.
No. 7, Main-street,
GIBRALTAR.

---

[192]The white Slaves of England compiled from Official documents with twelve spirited illustrations by James Cobden, Miller, Orton & Mulligan, 1853 pg124

[193] The Cruise Steam Yacht North Star: England, Russia, Denmark, France, Spain, Italy, ' Malta, Turkey, Madeira, ETC. REV. John Overton Choules, D.D.: James Blackwood, Paternoster Row. London 1854.

But after Colt's sudden death in 1862, his factory was run by his wife and soon there were many trails like the trail of tears, which started in Pennsylvania. In 1855 Blacks were forced out of Seneca Village in Manhattan, New York, now Central Park. One of the most advanced early settlements in the country, with the first public schools, churches, and other signatures of their development. In 1860

Africans were still being drafted to serve in New England despite regulations against African immigrants, but in 1863 a mob of Whites started draft riots in New York, they burned their settlements and killed over a thousand people. Then the city of Chambersburg Pennsylvania, with its banks and thriving businesses was burned to the ground, after the residents refused to pay a ransom of 100,000 in Gold. Stephen Smith 1795-1873 from Columbia, one of the wealthiest men of the era, and one of the conductors of the *underground railroad*, began recruiting people from the South. These were the incidents which lead to the civil war.

Figure 64 the burning of Chambersburg PA on July 30, 1864

Soldiers were being recruited as knights around the world. The British and Americans continued to stop their immigration from the source. Samuel W Baker, traveled to East Africa in 1861, he noticed of [194]"The Latookas, infinite care is bestowed upon the hair, which is trained to grow into the shape of a helmet, the perfecting of which requires unremitting attention for eight or ten years. This description closely resembles the headdress of the Ottoman soldiers and the "roundheads" of English soldiers". Their weapons consist of the lance, a powerful iron-headed mace, a long-bladed knife, and an ugly iron bracelet, armed with knife-blades.

Figure 65 Ottoman soldiers during the Crimean War, wore their hats like the Latookas, described by Baker. Library of Congress

---

[194] James William Buel Fighting in Africa: England's Battles with the Boers in the Transvaal, Including an Exhaustive History of the Settlement of Cape Colony, Wars with the Kaffirs, Matabeles, Zulus, the Diamond and Gold Mines of South Africa and a History of Exploration, Discovery, Conquest and Development by All the Famous Travelers that Have Traversed the Dark Continent ... (Baker pg125)

65

Figure 66 a) Benjamin Franklin in Ottoman headdress b) African recruit to Russia c) "Trading Places."

Then when the m*issionary* spy, David Livingston, arrived at Zanzibar in 1866, the [195]Arabs... were unfriendly to his purposes. "The Arabs were all dressed in their finery, and the slaves, in fantastic costumes, flourished swords, fired guns, and yelled vociferously." Why was there such a demand for slaves and who was he referring to as Arabs?

Figure 67 Arabian Sultans Tippu Tip and Said Ali Bin Said with identical attire to the trader Samuel Slater.

Figure 68 Bashi-bazouk soldiers from 1855 against Russian invasion

In 1869 Henry Stanley, went to the then Tanganyika to find Livingston after he went missing. He noted that, [196]were it not for their chains it would have been difficult to discover master from slave: their physiognomic traits were alike. What were they building which may have required this much human labor? Why would slaves who by definition, are held against their will, be furnished with swords and guns?

---

[195] James William Buel Fighting in Africa: England's Battles with the Boers in the Transvaal, Including an Exhaustive History of the Settlement of Cape Colony, Wars with the Kaffirs, Matabeles, Zulus, the Diamond and Gold Mines of South Africa and a History of Exploration, Discovery, Conquest and Development by All the Famous Travelers that Have Traversed the Dark Continent ...148

[196] James William Buel Fighting in Africa: England's Battles with the Boers in the Transvaal, Including an Exhaustive History of the Settlement of Cape Colony, Wars with the Kaffirs, Matabeles, Zulus, the Diamond and Gold Mines of South Africa and a History of Exploration, Discovery, Conquest and Development by All the Famous Travelers that Have Traversed the Dark Continent ...291

After the war ended, many retired officers returned to New England to find that things had changed dramatically. Suddenly those who were inviting Blacks into New England, found that their lives were in jeopardy. Augustus Washington, the early photographer or daguerreotypist and Attorney, was among the leaders now advocating an exodus to Liberia. The Northern states were now over taken by Jeffersonian politicians. Once the soldiers left Connecticut to help their fellows in the South, their places were taken over. By the late 1850s, writers were busy writing them out of the history books; but needed first to explain the presence of Black governors in New England.

Figure 69 29th Regiment of CT soldiers on their way South 1863 one of the last all Black footguards to the governor

[197]"Black governor for the whites, Reader-no-but a chief executive Black officer among the Blacks for themselves! For many years previous to the American Revolution down nearly to 1820, and perhaps a little later- it was the custom of the Negroes in *imitation* of the whites, to elect a governor for themselves."

[198]"The Black governor was of course exclusively of moral kind. He settled all grave disputes in the last resort; questioned conduct, and imposed penalties…" These historians claimed that Black governors presided over slaves, at a time and in a place of no large-scale commerce. A list of the names of these fictitious governors was then provided with no

Figure 70 An image of a Black angel still found in the stained-glass building on Prospect St in downtown Hartford, CT

historical precedence. The vital records of the state from 1700-1850, which would have provided an ethnographic portrait of the early governors also mysteriously vanished. The library of congress was set on fire once again in 1850, as the new leaders found that the story had been changing so dramatically that many references to the old world could now be erased. The idea that slavery was such a major industry in New England is also very ahistorical.

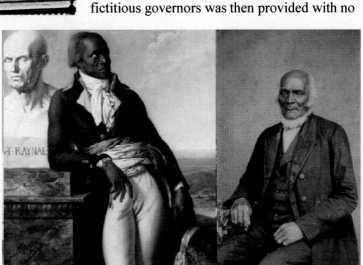

Figure 71 Girodet Trioson Jean Baptiste Belley Alias Mars; was a contemporary of Harriet Beecher Stowe

[197] Hartford in the olden time: its first thirty years, by Scæva, ed. by W.M.B. Hartley 1853 pg. 37
[198] The Knickerbocker; Or, New-York Monthly Magazine, Volume 42 1853 pg. 263

This revisionist idea was written at the same time that Stowe, a Connecticut native, illustrated the difference in the States as a result of slavery.

[199]Freedom is attended by intelligence, industry, and prosperity: and slavery brings with it ignorance, indolence, and poverty. Nothing shows this to be true so clearly as the contrast between the present condition of the great state of Virginia and the small state of Massachusetts. Both were settled by people from our country, and nearly at the same time." If the governor was elected by the wealthy citizens, then Black governors could not have been an anomaly in these states.

On 24 October 1915 the Hartford Courant featured an article about, "The Colored People Who Live in Hartford" As a small group that had been near extinction. The paper seemed to be trying to bury the history of Blacks in the region. There was no mention of prominent members of the Talcott Street Church, like Holdredge Primus, who became a wealthy gold prospector in California or the Yale graduate James Pennington who pastored the church among others.

Figure 72 Gold Street in Hartford late nineteenth century, part of the Black community in the city.

Washington D.C

Figure 73 Black development in DC in the nineteeth century

Figure 74 Freedman's Saving Bank, on Pennsylvania Ave in DC now site of US treasury Annex

Many Blacks resisted the push and remained in the stronghold of the nation's capital. The Freedman's Hospital was established in 1862 and the Freedman's Saving Bank was established in Pennsylvania in 1865; but moved its headquarters to Washington DC in 1868. With 37 branches in 17 states run by Blacks, this was the first multi-state bank in the nation. At this time, Trains, mechanical machinery, electricity and advanced methods of communication like the telephone and telegram were all coming into this New Order, as a direct consequence of an increase in the number of people now allowed to participate in the economy.

---

[199] A New Geography for Children by Harriet Beecher Stowe Sampson Low, 1855 pg. 135

Oklahoma

For those who had moved to Oklahoma, it [200]soon became one of the model states for Blacks. By 1865, African Americans founded more than 50 Black settlements, more than any other state. As these prospered, Black leaders successfully recruited Blacks by advertising, a "promised land" of business wealth and safety. Farming and ranching gave birth to the entertainment of Cowboy culture, as cowboys like Bill Pickett, were part of travelling attractions which toured internationally. Wild West stories grew from stories of Federal marshals like Bass Reeves, the inspiration for the characters of, The Lone Ranger, True Grit, and Django Unchained. Although president Harrison opened the territory for Whites in 1889 and 50,000 lined up, pushing the Blacks into less fertile areas. "By 1905 African-American farmers owned about 1.5 million acres, valued at 11 million dollars. More land was owned in total by African Americans here than across the entire United States."

Today [201] the Chickasaw Nation remains the most financially successful tribe in the country with the only Bank in the country wholly owned by a tribe. But in 1905 a Rockefeller Company, discovered Oil in one of these less fertile regions, and many Blacks were instant proprietors of this envied territory. One young Black girl, Sarah Rector whose parents had allotted some land to, became an overnight millionaire. Across the country laws were passed to deny parents automatic legal guardianship of their children and placed them in the custody of Whites. Twenty-five boarding schools were set up, housing an estimated 25,000 children, to educate them into their place in the new world order. By October 1913 there were already many petitions for guardianship of Sarah, including one from a man named Ed Sweeney. W.E.B Dubois and other prominent Blacks like Booker T Washington protested, but many of the land owners mysteriously disappeared. Tulsa was a quickly progressing region, with ten thousand Black residents surrounding Greenwood Ave, the center of culture and commerce. In 1921, Tulsa police deputized members of the lynch mob. Homes and businesses were looted, and many drive by shootings were reported. Planes dropped fire from the air and in the end Greenwoods' 40 square Blocks were little more than ashes and rubble and Blacks were forced to uproot once again.

Illinois

Among the French soldiers to immigrate to America, to fight alongside the Americans was Jean Du Sable. Du Sable settled at a place called Eschicago in 1779 and built his trading post there. This became the rest point and major trading station for trappers to sell their furs and buy supplies. There DuSable built houses, barns and smoke houses to cure meat. This was the beginning of the booming and thriving new settlement now called Chicago. An influx of Blacks traded Jeffersonian repression in Virginia, to settle in Illinois. During this time, some of the five percent who fled Europe, ended up in this region. Men like Polish general Kosciusko immigrated to Chicago, after being defeated by Napoleonic forces in 1794. President Thomas Jefferson's campaign for education as a tool to uplift the masses, was appealing to Kosciusko who left Jefferson as executor of his estate specifically to ensure the education of Blacks, but Jefferson never fulfilled this promise. In 1814 Edward Cole from the very wealthy Cole family, sent Thomas Jefferson a letter urging for the abolition of slavery. He then moved to Illinois with all his relatives and friends and set up each family on 160 acres of land. By 1818 Illinois became a state

---

[200]Long road to liberty Oklahoma's African American history and Culture Oklahoma Tourism and recreation department. Oklahoma City OK.
[201] National Conference on Undergraduate Research University of Central Oklahoma 2018 p58

and Cole, became its first governor. Coles' son Edward Coles, Jr. may possibly be the grandfather or relative of Nat King Cole.

Chicago was the Black frontier, as the population grew from an exodus of Blacks leaving the South. This mass migration was a catalyst in the development of the railroad system. Men like Granville T Woods (1856-1910) and Elijah McCoy (1844-1928), were among the pioneers who helped develop the railway system around this time, but Woods was later driven out of Chicago because of the targeted efforts to destroy any Black progress. His many inventions, brought electrical and telegraphic wiring through trains in New York. He was forced to sue Thomas Edison for infringement of his patent rights twice and won both times; but the fight against white unscrupulousness was exhausting. Frank Mc Worter (1777-1854) a gunpowder merchant, founded New Philadelphia on 80 acres in 1836, but the town's population was driven out, and today remains abandoned. In 1837 Elijah Lovejoy, editor of the Observer, was killed and his press destroyed.

Another great Chicagoan, Lewis Latimer, was the only man then, to have written a book detailing the technological mechanics of incandescent lighting. Since Latimer's name appears on the patent, he is given credit for organizing the legal paper work for Thomas Edison and Bell Labs, but as the sole author of the design, he must have been the inventor, whose work became the property of others. A notice appeared in Frederick Douglas' North Star, which petitioned for his freedom in 1847. McCoy an engineer who graduated in Scotland as a Master Mechanic, moved to Michigan where he eventually patented many devices and established his own lubricating company in 1920, but was struck by a car and died shortly after. The greatest damage came from fires, like The Great Chicago Fire of 1871 and communities around lake Michigan, from Urbana to port Heron that same day. [202] The Chicago Historical society which began in 1851, had 17,000 volumes of its books and collections destroyed in the fire of 1871 and about 100 thousand were left homeless. This sparked another great migration of Blacks to aid in the recovery. Within twenty years, Daniel Hale Williams opened a medical school and established the fourth hospital in the US, Provident Hospital in 1891. He became the first person ever to perform a successful open-heart surgery. Oscar Micheaux, founded Micheaux Film and Book Company in Chicago. His film "The

Figure 75 Members of South Carolina Legislature 1862

Homesteader," was released shortly after Griffin's "Birth of a nation," in 1915. The two films symbolize the sharp cultural contrast, between Whites versus Blacks. While Griffin's rallied for an awakened barbarian, Micheaux's ordinary man, echoed the frustration of generations to come, [203]"Can I Live."

The Carolinas

[204]By the time of the American Revolution half the population of Virginia were Black, and in the Carolinas, it was two Blacks to one White. After being pushed out of Philadelphia, and with an influx of white immigrants into New England many wealthy Blacks began moving South and West.

[202] Histoire des États-Unis, C.F. Chamerot, 1894 pg. 124
[203] Songwritter Jay Z
[204] Alistair Cooke's America, Alfred A knopf INc, New York 1973 Borzoi Books p 191

[205]Charleston and New Orleans particularly, were centers of free Negro workers in skilled trades, and both cities had a considerable number of well-educated Blacks. [206]North Carolina had the first state university in 1789, and there were more mills and furniture factories, there than any other state. (Still in 1908) some sections, few White people live, and we see Black faces almost entirely, more than half the people in this state were negroes." This was home to men like Thomas Day (1801-1861) among the dying caste of African Americans, who kept the legacy of quality carpentry and the tradition of quality furniture from the Carolinians. John Jones (1817-1879) was a wealthy tailor who later moved to Chicago. There was a Henry Blair (1834), who patented a seed planting machine, possibly the same Henry Blair (1834-1920 who was congressman in New Hampshire. These may have been related to James Blair (1788-1841) a wealthy plantation owner in the West Indies. William Ellison (1790-1861) a cotton gin maker and Blacksmith, owned 40 slaves and 1000 acres of land and fought on the side of the confederate army to maintain his slaves as property.

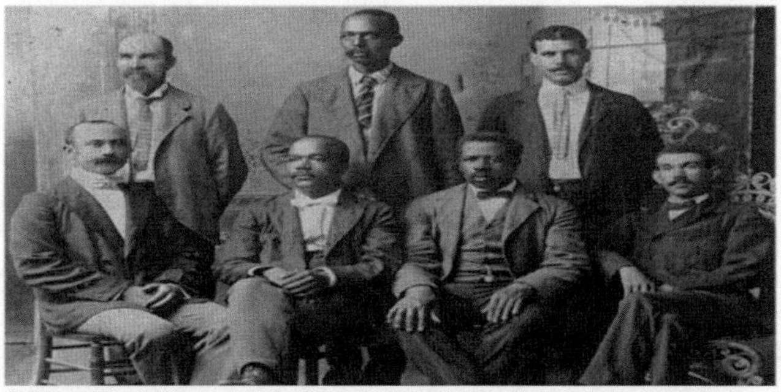

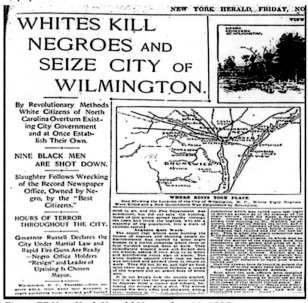

Figure 76 B) Above right Some of the Founders of Mechanics & Farmers Bank in 1900. J. A. Dodson, J. R. Hawkins, John Merrick, Aaron M. Moore, W.G. Pearson, James E. Shepard, G. W. Stephens, and Stanford L. Warren Durham County Library: http://durhamcountylibrary.org/exhibits/dhpa/photo_archives/c/c0 60.php 1/3/17

Figure77 New York Herald November 11, 1898

Richard B Fitzgerald (1843-1918) moved from Delaware to North Carolina to establish Coleman Manufacturing Company in 1897, another of the first cotton mills, also owned and operated by Blacks. Fitzgerald also owned a very profitable brickmaking business. His bricks were used for major construction projects in the state's largest cities, including the capital. He and eight other businessmen started the Mechanics and Farmers Bank, one of the first banks in Durham North Carolina, just a few years after the Capital Savings Bank in Washington. The Carolinas had the highest Black legislative representation and were a very real threat to White Supremacy, until 1865 when the capital was burned. By 1880 the remaining Black politicians in the Carolinas were driven underground. Then in 1898 "Whites kill Negroes and seize city of Wilmington." Willmington was the same blueprint used for every city in America. As went Willington, so did Tulsa, Manhattan, Philadelphia, Kansas, San Francisco, Chicago, Hartford, Boston, Providence and so on. Then the new rulers-maintained power by imposing heavy taxes and confiscated millions of dollars of property. They then pioneered the new government backed slave trade in the form of incarceration. The prisons were so crowded and in such deplorable conditions that, [207]"a number of

[205] A Pictorial History of Black Americans, 5th revised edition by Langston Hughes, Milton Meltzer, and C. Eric Lincoln. Crown Publishers New York 1983
[206] The book of Knowledge, Arthur Mee, Holland Thomson etal. 1908 p 5983-6
[207] Report and Resolutions of State Officers, Board and Committees to the General Assembly of the State of South Carolina. Volume II South Carolina, General Assembly 1891 pg 573

prisoners have come and died, without ever having done any kind of work... It must be remembered, too, that consumption in its different forms, scrofula and syphilis, are the curses of the negro race: and unless they changed their modes of life, these diseases will be sufficient to settle the race problem." Later, Black men were deliberately infected with syphilis, and then the American government's Center for Disease Control, pretended to be treating them while studying their deterioration, in the infamous Tuskegee experiment in Alabama.

Alabama and Mississippi

Figure 78 A government official from the Centers for Disease Control, inserting needle into unsuspecting man.

When Alabama became a state in 1819, Horace King built an impressive 32,000 square-foot cotton warehouse and is [208]"credited with designing and managing the construction of many bridges in Alabama, Georgia and Mississippi. He also built the Alabama State Capitol building, which was burned in 1849 and served in the Alabama State legislature after the civil war." The cast iron bridge was probably invented after many of these bridges were burned. One of the first cast iron bridges in the world, was built in Senegal, shortly afterwards. In 1859 Planters in Georgia defied Jefferson's ruling and managed to transport 300 Negroes on the Wanderer from the Congo to Georgia and that same year, a little over a hundred to Alabama on the Cotilda. They called their town in Mobile Alabama, Africa Town. Entire families labored together in the textile mills of Georgia and the Carolinas. Historians tend to connect the existence of Black Americans to the invention of the cotton Gin; but the fact is cotton did not become a major production until after the prohibition imposed by Jefferson on Black immigrants in 1808. Many if not most of the cotton plantations were owned by Blacks who were among the ones rejecting abolition, because of the high price which they paid to bring people to the country. They were part of the Old-World thinkers, who did not realize the big picture and the racial caste, which would later enslave their children. A survey of the Alabama and Mississippi, as late as 1908, found that [209] more than half the population of Mississippi was composed of Negroes and in Alabama, there were still "plantations where hundreds of Negroes worked. In some counties, they outnumbered Whites 5 to 1. Mobile was once part of Louisiana," but gerrymandering techniques were used to redraw the map and reduce Louisiana's Black representation.

Virginia

Virginia and Tennessee have suffered the most extensive record loss from arson. In 1902, Maggie Walker (1864-1934) opened the Penny Savings Bank of Virginia. Two years later, Henry Boyd (1876-1959) son of General Assembly member John Boyd (1841-1885) established the Cent Saving Bank in Tennessee.

Ireland

Until the 19th century [210]"The Scots inhabiting the northern parts of (Scotland) were Black."

THE Natives here are very well proportioned, being generally black of Complection, and free from bodily imperfections. They speak the *Irish* Language, and wear the Plade, Bonnet, &c. as other Islanders.

[208] A history of Architecture in the Americas, Cardinal-Pett, Clare Routledge, 2015 pg 243

[209] The book of Knowledge, Arthur Mee, Holland Thomson etal. 1908 p 5983-6

[210] A Description of the Western Islands of Scotland: Containing a Full Account of Their Situation, Extent, Soils, Products, Harbours, Bays... With a New Map of the Whole, ... To which is Added a Brief Description of the Isles of

The Plaid bonnet now associated with the Scots and Irish was the traditional dress of the Maasai at least by this time, according to H. B. Stowe's description in Uncle Tom's Cabin. Blacks lived throughout Scotland and Ireland and some of the Jews who immigrated to the US were among the founders of the Seventh Day Adventist Church, for Jewish Christians. Among these were Ellen G White, who referred to this gilded era as the "great controversy" between the devil and God. This generation believed that they were witnessing the obvious release of the Devil onto Earth.

In 1844 about a million-people were left to starve to death in Ireland. The population were land locked, and their ground poisoned. Meanwhile in 1844, in the Irish dominated suburbs of Kensington, several city blocks were burned. [211]John Curran an Irish attorney pleaded with the British parliament to help his people who he referred to as the 'Western Negros.' Then whatever records were left of the many absentee, landholding, nobility who fled, was later destroyed in 1922, when the Public records office of Ireland was burned down.

The Western Frontier

Figure 79 Governor of California Pio Pico 1833 b) Biddy Mason nurse, real-estate investor and founder of California AME c) Alexander Leidesdorff

In 1844 Alexander Leidesdorff set out to establish the state of California, he launched the first ever steamboat to sail on San Francisco Bay and built a warehouse and the first hotel there. In 1845 James Pierce Beckworth found the shortcut through the Sierra Nevada in his expedition to find gold. Leidesdorff was [212]owner of many city lots about 35,000 acres, which after the discovery of gold became of immense value. This led to an even greater influx of speculators. After his sudden death in 1848, and his property burned in 1851, without a will, probably due to its destruction by fire, his mother from St.Croix, contested the transfer of his property unsuccessfully against a man ironically named Joseph Folsome. California finally achieved Statehood after an influx of many foreign speculators, and by [213]1863 Nevada already had a large foreign-born population of Yugoslavs and Basques; but there has been considerable record loss because of fires. The library of congress was set on fire once again in 1850, and Virginia City in 1875, as the new leaders found that the story had been changing so dramatically that many references to the old world could now be erased. Besides the "considerable" loss of records, there were also overt fabrications. [214]From the 19th and early 20th centuries, news wasn't reported, it was unscrupulously manufactured. The

Orkney, and Schetland written By, Martin and published by Andrew Bell, at the Cross-Keys and Bible, in Cornhil, near Stocks-Market., 1703 pg158-240

[211] Speeches of John Philpot Curran, Esq: With the Speeches of Grattan, Erskine and Burke. To which is Prefixed, A Brief Sketch of the History of Ireland, and Also a Biographical Account of Mr. Curran, Volume 1 John Philpot Curran, Henry Grattan, Thomas Erskine Baron Erskine, Edmund Burke I. Riley, 1809

[212] Quarterly of the California Historical Society Vol VII No.2 L Leidesdorff-Folsome estate June 1928

[213] Eicholz, Alice, PHD. Ancestry's Red Book, American State, County & Town Sources.1992 Pg. 454, 468,471,

[214]Calkins Carroll. Etal, The Story of America, Readers Ass. Inc Pleasantville NY Digest 1975 p.364

growing awareness that these actions were coordinated, led the government to appoint Frederick Douglas as the first national registrar or recorder of deeds.

The following table shows the aggregate population of the United States at each census from 1790 to 1890, together with the rate of increase during each decade:

CENSUS YEARS.	Population.	Per cent of increase.
1790..	3,029,214	....
1800..	5,308,483	35.10
1810..	7,239,881	36.38
1820..	9,633,822	33.07
1830..	12,866,020	33.55
1840..	17,069,453	32.67
1850..	23,191,876	35.87
1860..	31,443,321	35.58
1870..	38,558,371	22.63
1880..	50,155,783	30.08
1890..	62,622,250	24.86

The population of the United States on June 1, 1890, as shown by the final count, exclusive of Indians and other persons in Indian territory, on Indian reservations, and in Alaska, was 62,622,250; including these persons the population was 62,979,766. In 1880 the population with the same exclusions was 50,155,783. The absolute increase of the population in the 10 years intervening was 12,466,467, and the percentage of increase was 24.86. In 1870 the population was stated as 38,558,371. According to these figures the absolute increase in the decade between 1870 and 1880 was 11,597,412, and the percentage of increase was 30.08.

Upon their face these figures show that the population increased 869,055 more between 1880 and 1890 than between 1870 and 1880, while the rate of increase has apparently diminished from 30.08 to 24.86 per cent. If these figures were derived from correct data, they would be disappointing. Such a reduction in the rate of increase, in the face of the heavy immigration during the past 10 years, would argue a diminution in the fecundity of the population, or a corresponding increase in its death rate. These figures are, however, easily explained when the character of the data used is understood. It is well known, the fact having been demonstrated by extensive and thorough investigation, that the census of 1870 was grossly deficient in the southern states, so much so as not only to give an exaggerated rate of increase of the population between 1870 and 1880 in these states, but to affect materially the rate of increase in the country at large.

These omissions were not the fault of the Census Office nor within its control. The census of 1870 was taken under a law which the Superintendent, General Francis A. Walker, characterized as "clumsy, antiquated, and barbarous". The Census Office had no power over its enumerators save a barren protest, and even this right was questioned in some quarters. In referring to these omissions the [215] Superintendent of the Tenth Census (1880) said in his report in relation to the taking

While emancipation was achieved through the collaboration between Blacks and Whites, it was only the motive of most fighters and abolitionists. For the politicians who garnered support for their own agendas, it was only a means to a greater end. This war had many sides, and people fought along the sides which served their best interest and to the extent that these interests were aligned; but very few saw the

---

[215] Department of Interior, Census Office Compendium of the Eleventh Census 1890 Part I-Population. Robert P. Porter Superintendent. Washington D.C. Government Printing Office 1892. Bureau of the Census Library.

big picture. Lincoln and many Whig-Federalists, realized that the freedom of the slaves, was imperative to increase their voter base and remain in power. While the Jeffersonians in the North could not allow the Blacks to build their own government. This would have left them in total ruin, since most of the trade was still with the West Indies and Africa. Haiti at this point was one of the leading markets in the world; so if Lincoln "could save the union without freeing any slave, he would do it." But the goal of Jeffersonian politicians was to destroy the emerging head of the southern states. In the end "the south was beaten, devastated and the cotton kingdom destroyed. General Sherman destroyed every town, rail yard, mansion and crop. A systematic atrocity…" that is hailed as a democratic victory, but was really another example of the agenda for targeted destruction of Blacks. The top ten percent were dramatically affected, and long after the war, a continuous stream of White immigrants, and relentless massacres and violence ended the Black majority in the South and eventually, diminished any prospect of their recovery.

Figure 80 The Sunday Magazine of New York World News Paper

Before the civil war two thirds of the population in the South were Black and possibly nearly as much over all. In 1780 the population in the US was about 2,000,000 and after Jefferson took office, there were strict immigration restrictions on Blacks, so in 1840 ships like the USS Creole on route to South Carolina and the Amistad to New England in 1844 were turned away. Ninety nine percent of the immigrants who came in, after Jefferson took office were White Europeans; and [216]of the 50,155,783-people recorded on the census of 1880, more than half had foreign born parents, more than 26,000,000 were the descendants of *recent White* European immigrants. Between 1861 and 1914 twenty-three million new immigrants arrived from Europe. Thus, even if African Americans represented only twenty-five to thirty percent of the population (12-15,000,000), it means that Whites had to have been the minority prior to the civil war, and the dynamics were only *recently* changed. At its peak in 1907 about three thousand people arrived each day at Ellis Island. The strategy of secret and subtle sabotage evolved, into a massive force and in 1866 the KKK like a malignant and invasive cell, metastasized throughout the country, destroying everything Black.

After [217]the civil war *six veterans* of the confederate army formed a secret organization called the Klu Klux Klan in 1866. They effectively terrorized Blacks and obstructed them from voting, so that by 1869, the Democratic Party, (White supremacist) control was reestablished in Tennessee in 1869 and other states soon followed. Back Once in power, White elite no longer needed the Klan, for suppression of Blacks could be accomplished by official, "legal" means. (13) White supremacists were the victors in what has been called the reconstruction war and, as usual, the victors wrote the history of the conflict. By 1900, a White supremacist interpretation of Reconstruction was generally accepted by White historians throughout the country. Estimates of its membership in the early 1920s range from 3 1/2 to 5 million members. Businessmen, clergy,

---

216 Webster's New International Dictionary of the English Language Based on the International Dictionary of 1890 and 1900: Now Completely Revised in All Departments, Including Also a Dictionary of Geography and Biography, Being the Latest Authentic Quarto Edition of the Merriam Series, Volume 1. G. & C. Merriam Company, 1926   XIX
217 *Violence, The Klu Klux Klan and the struggle for equality. An informational and instructional kit*. The Connecticut Education Association, The council on interracial Books for children and the National Education Association. May 1981

public officials, judges, police and other "respectable" members of communities were the mainstay of the Klan in the 1920's.

These respectable members of society worked within the population, with their hoods in place. They may have concealed their identities but not their agenda. In response to Black protests, the new rulers reluctantly conceded to Black education. But they controlled the narrative, so that much of what is taught has its roots in this official agenda at a new more effective form of intellectual subjugation, a sort of [218]"mental slavery." This is when the term "Niger" began to be used with contempt, and sarcasm. This is also the time when the documents relating to the early government began to surface.

Figure 81 Created by Currier & Ives in 1872, the same company which created caricatures of Blacks as apes. What is misleading about the image is the fact that these men were representatives of regions which were often newly established and among the first representatives Ever, for their states; but this is a deliberate misrepresentation of the many Blacks who were part of congress.

Andrew Johnson, who replaced the assassinated Abraham Lincoln quickly went to work to reverse the progress which Lincoln had made for Blacks. He transferred more than seven million dollars to Russia, in 1867, under the guise of an Alaskan purchase. This purchase was so insignificant to any American plan for expansion, that no president ever set foot in Alaska, until over a half century later. Early census records also reveal that the inhabitants of Alaska like Louisiana were mostly Creoles.

Johnson handed out thousands of pardons to confederate leaders, while congress was on vacation, and facilitated the Black codes which legalized discrimination and brutality against them. He accomplished this through the KKK which ravaged Black communities. By the end of his presidency, many Black cities, were destroyed and gerrymandering techniques redrew the map to disenfranchise their elections.

Figure 75 Newspapers published these caricatures of the Blacks, many now stranded and without homes.

After White Supremacists took over the South and *liberated* the slaves, they brought in a steady stream of White immigrants and soon took control of the legislature, and all aspects of economic or political power. The Black majority in the Southern States was over turned, and the supremacist began to erect monuments all over their new territories to commemorate their victories. From 1867 to 1967, the [219]Nadir of suffering and discrimination swept through the country and the entire globe. White supremacists were unleashed throughout the world and the spread of their socio-pathology ensued. At this time oppression came in the form of Jim Crow laws and Black codes. After the white soldiers assumed legitimate command of the military and police, slavery was substituted with incarceration and plantations with prisons, where the new

[218]Term coined by Jamaican singer Bob Marely.
[219] James Weldon Johnson coined the term

masters, were prison owners who thrived on new systems of enslavement. Soon black soldiers were held as *prisoners* of war and others went underground and started to turn on each other. Some killings labelled as gang related, were actually organized to spread rumors of hysteria, mistrust and anxiety, among the Blacks. It is no wonder that Americans in this era moved to the beat of the depressing, sultry sound of the Blues. Once cornered with nowhere to run, the negro spiritual as sung by the Fisk Jubilee singers, cautioned them to, *"wait in the water, until God troubles the water."* This pause lasted nearly a century, until the tune finally began to change after the civil rights era.

Figure 83 The Jubilee Singers 1871

Figure 84 Newark New Jersey 1967, by Don Hogan New York Times

The essence of Black protests have come down to us as riots, but these citizens saw their Black merchants one by one suffer complete bankruptcy and disruption. In their stead came anyone else, Chinese, Indians, and Germanic or Russian Jews, all came to replace them. Their response, was to purge everything with a new fire. The usurpers, had now taken England, France and America, and transferred large numbers of Germans to Brazil and South Africa; but tried unsuccessfully to take the Caribbean islands. They now turned to Africa, and the remaining strongholds of the Ottomans, to uproot the Blacks once and for all.

A Survey of the Old World

A Discourse in the systematic destruction of the Creoles, Moors, Jews and other Black identities.

Figure 85 a) Ivan IV 1530-1584 first Czar of Russia. b) Early 18th century painting Peter the Great, Tsar of Russia (1672–1725), by the German artist Baron Gustav von Mardefeld. At the battlefield and are wearing ceremonial dress. and Moorish boy believed to be Gannibal.c) Abram Petrovich Gannibal (1696-1781) d) Alexander Sergeevich Pushkin (1799-1837)

At this time the Blacks who could afford to run, left for Liberia, the Caribbean and some returned to Eastern European and Mediterranean regions, where the Old-World Powers continued to hold on. Prussia was home to a large and affluent Black minority, and MonteNegro was founded around 1850. Russia had a large [220]Black aristocracy, like the Zingani or Zingano [221]"of brown complexion with somewhat coarse hair of coal black hue, many of them inhabit large and handsome houses in Moscow, appear abroad in elegant equipages, and are scarcely to be distinguished from the upper classes of the Russians, unless, indeed by possessing superior personal advantages and mental accomplishments." Black sailors and celebrities navigated the globe and stars like American Ira Aldridge, a famous actor of the day, were among the people, living and travelling throughout Europe. Aldridge was killed in Poland in 1867.

Of immense height, with black hair and dark skin, he was not handsome. "Dreadful and repulsive in appearance," according to one of his relations, Berezin, with whom Thiébaut, the author of the well-known memoirs, had some conversation at Berlin. One-eyed and squinting, as we know, he was knock-kneed as well. And he himself was far from anxious to leave his face for the inspection of posterity. "Prince Patiomkin," writes Catherine, in one of her letters to Grimm, "has never

122   *CATHERINE THE GREAT*

consented to be painted, and if there exists any portrait or silhouette of him, it is against his wish." In 1783, however, he gives way to the wish of the Empress, and it is in this year that he sits for the full-length portrait which is now to be seen in the Salle des Maréchaux of the Winter Palace at St Petersburg · an official portrait

When Markham, and his team visited Russia they [222]"were much struck by observing an alter on one side of the entrance, with candles burning on it, and the picture of a saint, *black, as usual*, and in a golden habit, before which the native merchants bowed and crossed themselves as they passed onward to

---

[220] The story of a throne Catherine ii of Russia p6 121-122,198,241, 252,323,399,400 (Excerpt in Photo Box above)

[221] Kingston, William Henry G. *The Circassian chief.* 1843 Page 274

[222] William Henry Kingston, G. *Fred Markham in Russia: Or, The Boy Travellers in the Land of the Czar.* Griffith and Farran, 1858 78,79 and 140 & 154-155

transact their affairs. Here were collected representatives of all nations, and from every part of Russia-a strange medley of physiognomies, tongues.... The object of the travelers, however, was to meet with the civilized specimens of the race of Zingari or Gypsy, whom they would find there. They were not long in discovering them as they moved about among the crowd. There was the same swarthy hue (dark complexion), black, burning eyes, and cunning, quick expression of countenance which distinguish them in every part of the world."

Figure 86 Women from the Black sea region of Crimea and Circassia late 19th century. Portraits of people with afros like these were probably replaced with halos

These people originated from, [223] Zingion on the coast of Africa...[224]The ancient name for Zanzibar and its people is zinj, and it is generally accepted that the name "Zanzibar" is derived from the Persian word "Zangh" meaning Negro and bar, a coast. Thus, the name in its widest sense signifies the Negro coast and the inhabitants..." Zanzibar's domain extended to Southern Arabia, including Yemen and Oman and this Persian-Omani connection dates back to the fourteenth century and possibly the Ottoman Empire. [225]Zanzibar became a port colony in 1503 and in the early 20th century, Rudyard Kipling witnessed that men were still being sent there to be trained into Admirals. This was a training base for Russian generals, so that Napoleon's first attempt to take Russia was foiled by these soldiers in 1812.

Abram Petrovitch Gannibal (1696-1781), was one of the generals from France, who fled to Russia, to become a General in that Army. But the Russian monarchy tried to increase the Aryan population and called for more Germans and [226]as an inducement to come to Russia, The Russian monarchy gave Germans about 160 acres and were settled upon large tracts of land in Southern Russia...During this period of increased Germanization, the monarchy orchestrated a great deal of censorship. Artist, journalists and writers like Gannibal's grandson Alexander Pushkin, lived under extreme repression. Pushkin was cognizant of the growing racial tensions and made every effort to assert his ethnicity amidst a heightened spirit of German nationalism. His writings express feelings of isolation, [227]"It is time to abandon the boring shore of elements hostile to me, and amid Southern billions under the sky of my Africa, to sigh for gloomy Russia, where I have suffered...loved...and buried my heart."

[223] The History of the Works of the Learned, or an Impartial account of Books lately printed in all parts of Europe, Volume 9 by H. Rhodes, 1707 The commission of Cosma of Egypt's Christian Typography. 131-134

[224] Steere, Edward A. C. Madan Society for Promoting Christian Knowledge A Handbook of the Swahili Language as Spoken at Zanzibar, 1884

[225] Kipling, Rudyard: Letters of Travel, Garden City New York. Doubleday, Page & Co. 1920

[226] State Historical Society of North Dakota, Collections, Volume 1 1906 p.199

[227] Pushkin, Aleksandr Eugene Onegin, Chapter 1 stanza 50, Pushkin

The new Americans with a simple hand shake and promised friendship, signed a treaty with Zanzibar in 1838, which allowed the two countries to trade peacefully. Within a few years after Livingston and Stanley came in to survey the land as peaceful missionaries, the country was attacked, invaded and destroyed.

Figure 87(Above) Zanzibar Palace LOC before destruction 1880 (Left) Palace after destruction in1889

Figure 88 Rudolf Ernst later exhibiting as Rodolphe Ernst was an Austrian-born orientalist painter in Paris (Vienna, 14 February 1854 - Fontenay-aux-Roses, 1932) 20th Century North Africa.

Figure 89. 1891 portrait of Mtesas and dignitaries from Die Volker der Erde, Wurzburg Vienna b) 19th century image of king toffa of the kingdom of Dahomey from Malerische Studien, Neuchatel

The goal was to destroy every element of the Old World, and in the process, they left a trail of death and destruction, that the world had never seen before. One of the cities which Livingston described as "so strongly built that it would require cannons to destroy," was Simbamwenni. It "contain(ed) a thousand houses, and a population of about 5,000." The name sounds very close to great Zimbabwe, but Zimbabwe is said to have been destroyed in the sixteenth century. Another city which fits this des Connecticut cription is Kiliwa. Kiliwa is also located in Tanzania near Zanzibar. It [228]became a major trading port in East Africa in the 1200s with many houses of stone and mortar, which now lay in ruins.

Figure 90 a) Kiliwa, 1572 by George Braun and b) Kiliwa now destroyed photo courtesy of UNESCO

---

[228] Simon Adams, John Briquebec, Ann Kramer. 1992 Illustrated Atlas of world History. pg. 100

End of the Old World.

At the close of nineteenth century, the population in Russia was exactly the opposite of the American population. The Slavs, were the "great," White Russians who were enslaved, by a very diverse ruling class; and [229]"according to the census of 1897, well over one-half of the population of Russia (56.7 percent) consisted of peoples other than the "Great" Russians. Except for the Siberian peoples and some

of the Tartars, all of these nationalities had become part of Russia, between the 1650s and 1890s." These were the Moors, Zinganis, Gypsies, Bohemians and Jews among others. Russia and Germany were not only racially diverse nations but represented a symbolic model for the equally diverse American population. A [230]"widely circulated Negro publication… (at the time, considered Russia), a country in which dozens of racial and lingual types have settled their differences and found common meeting ground…and racial tolerance and peace now exist."

Figure 91 Painting by Gyula Tornai_The_Connoisseurs 1892

This diversity was a real problem for the Russian Czar, Nicholas II (1894-1918). He [231]"attempted to establish Russian nationality throughout his vast domains and therefore suppressed the local institutions and as far as possible, the various national groups which went to make up his empire." He was well aware that, [232] "his power rested on precarious grounds and knew that he was in the power of his own nobles. To liberate himself, he endeavored to weaken if not destroy the old nobility. First by leading them into all sorts of extravagance, and then by creating a new order between nobles and peasants who should feel that they owed their elevation entirely to him." It is a significant reminder, that this noble class were [233] "landowners, frequently of a different nationality from the common people, (who) retained their traditional rights, as did the cities, and were often assimilated into the Russian *ruling* class." Among these were the Zinganis, Moors and many other groups of Black people. A steady flow of African soldiers were dispatched to Russian and Prussian territory, but the Russian Monarchy had a powerful, secret ally to help eliminate them. Andrew Johnson, who replaced the assassinated Abraham Lincoln transferred more than seven million dollars to Russia, in 1867, under the guise of an Alaskan purchase. The KKK rose to power as a civil miltary which drove the Black federal marshals out and these assasins became the new national guards. The British-American campaign against slavery was simply a measure to stop the traffic of these soldiers who seemed to arrive as perpetual reinforcement.

---

[229] Lederer, Ivo J. Russian Foreign Policy Essays in Historical Perspective New Haven and London University Press. (as represented by R.A. Fadeev's Opinion on the Eastern Question and N. Ia. Danilevskii's Russia and Europe published in 1869) 26 Russian Foreign Policy.

[230] Special to the New York Times. "Feds are working among Negroes." Widespread Propaganda by Radical Leaders Known to the Government. New York Times October 19, 1919

[231] G. & C. Merriam Company, Webster's New International Dictionary of the English Language Based on the International Dictionary of 1890 and 1900: Volume I 1926 137-138 National histories

[232] Kingston, William Henry. *Giles Fred Markham in Russia: Or, The Boy Travellers in the Land of the Czar.* Griffith and Farran, 1858 143-144

[233] Lederer, Ivo J. Russian Foreign Policy Essays in Historical Perspective New Haven and London University Press (as represented by R.A. Fadeev's Opinion on the Eastern Question and N. Ia. Danilevskii's Russia and Europe published in 1869) 28 Russian Foreign Policy.

Figure 92 Samuel Colt 1814-1862

Samuel Colt's revolver, revolutionized the war and enabled the American civil war, but that victory was as brief as his life. This was only the beginning of the most highly industrialized and technologically advanced warfare, that the world had ever known. From the 1930s through the end of WWII in 1947, over 30 million people were deliberately wiped out from Nazi and Soviet occupied territories. The casualties of this era surpassed entire millennia of Earth's population. Based on the population in Russia today, it is possible to deduce that the genocides purged the Black Russians from the country.

Figure 93 Black/Swarthy Russian Soldiers

Figure 94 New York Times article July, 30 1909

In 1909 the New York Times reported that, [234]"the Moors were directing a fierce attack against the Spanish garrison;" Observations at Melilla show the army numbers 50,000, in strong position." Until the first World War, the Ottomans maintained defense of the Mediterranean, Caribbean islands and some of the areas in Europe that were still connected to the Old World.

When the Titanic debuted, from the White Star Line in 1914, it was a direct threat to this monopoly of the seas. This may have been the cause for its sinking, and the trigger of World War One, three years later. On May 7th 1915, a torpedo fired at the Lusitania, on route from New York to Liverpool. Within minutes the ship sank and nearly twelve hundred people were killed.

At this time, Russia was said to have had the largest Jewish population of any country in the world. Many of these Jews were also very White, the small exception to the Jewish identity of the preceding century and probably the only ones spared. [235]"The Czar's Jewish subjects (were) confined by law, to a definite part of the empire, known as the Pale of

Figure 95 Mauretania 1906

---

[234] The New York Times Traveler, By William S. Niederkorn, 8/12,1909
[235] Ibid. 26 Russian Foreign Policy.

Settlement (or ghettos). The Pale proper, wherein all the Russian Jews dwell comprises the entire territory of Russian Poland and two-thirds of the entire population." Two thirds of the population were held in confinement and the officers responsible for confining them were the Aryan minority. Then [236]as an inducement to come to Russia, The Russian monarchy gave German farmers about 160 acres and were settled upon large tracts of land in Sothern Russia... On [237]"October 31, 1915, Jewish relief societies reported that in territory swept by Germans 150,000 Russian Jews are without means of support, homeless and starving... that same year anti-German mobs protested in Moscow" It is from this background that Lenin, Trotsky and the Bolsheviks (the majority), usurped power, assassinated the Russian royal family and moved the capital back to Moscow in 1917.

Lenin adopted Karl Marx's' communist manifesto, and the belief that, "religion was the opium to the masses;" so Lenin's Bolsheviks and Black hundreds made the fatal error of positioning themselves as the militant Godless. Lenin studied the pattern of these revolutions and realized that history had shown how, "the better organized more politically conscious minority forced its will upon the majority and defeated it." His first actions were to remove all civil and political disadvantages of the Jews, repeal all laws abridging religious freedom, institute reforms including freedom of speech, call on Blacks around the world to form communist governments and to eject the foreign philanthropists who controlled many of their national industries and land, and his administration began to encourage the emigration of Blacks from America to Russia. Cuba adopted this policy, and seized control of all the foreign owned structures

Figure 96 Marcus Garvey

in their country. Then on [238]"July 29, 1918, Lenin declared informally that a state of war existed between Russia and the Allies." At that time the U.S. under President Wilson, granted partial recognition to the new Russian government, but [239]the proposed recognition of Lenin caused "consternation." This league of nations, was like a Black league. Joining it would have legitimized the Bolsheviks and maintained the relics of Black power as a direct attack on the emerging Aryan super power. By the fall of that year, the influenza virus spread like wildfire throughout the world, claiming the lives of over thirty million people. The virus apparently did not disrupt Lenin's operations, because by 1919 the Bolsheviks recaptured the Riga line. Anglo-American journalists were becoming increasingly worried about the Russian communist objectives and their affiliation with "Black Power" movements in America. [240]While Old World journalists in France recognized that they were "faced with a vast effort to establish Anglo-Saxon supremacy in the world." According to German news source, Kreuz Zeitung, "The Anglo-Saxons are leagued against the French."

An October 1919, New York Times titled, "Feds are working among Negroes," sounded the alarm that Russian Leaders Lenin and Trotsky were "being circulated among negroes in all parts of the country... The principle agencies are Negro magazines and so-called "negro betterment organizations,"

[236] State Historical Society of North Dakota, Collections, Volume 1 1906 p.199
[237] Webster's New International Dictionary of the English Language, Based on the International Dictionary of 1890 and 1900: Volume 1. G. & C. Merriam Company, 1926 137-138
[238] Tumulty, Joseph P. *Woodrow Wilson as I Know Him*. Garden City, NY: Doubleday, Page, 1921.pg. 523
[239] *Woodrow Wilson as I Know Him*. Tumulty, Joseph P. Garden City, NY: Doubleday, 1921.
[240] The Literary Digest for 9/28/1929: Foreign Comment *European Tremors at McDonald's vist* p. 16-17

84

like (Garvey's paper, "The Negro World."). The article outlined snippets of the propaganda being circulated in Negro papers. This propaganda ultimately led to the defeat of President Wilson's endorsed successor and his vision of peace, by joining their League of Nations. The American public became aroused by the idea that the Bolshevik extremists were funding this uprising of American Blacks. Under the heading, 'Sedition, Syndicalism, Sabotage and Anarchy,' Congress reviewed reports of these allegations.[241]"Several Negroes were selected… and transported to Moscow, where they were given thorough instructions in the operation and theories of communism." The Negro leaders of this scheme were Richard B. Moore, and Lovett Fort-Whiteman of Chicago."

Lenin worked to develop Russia's infrastructure by building the trans-Siberian railroad system and invited Black American engineers to aid it this effort. These immigrants weren't charity cases, they came with the very important job of helping to develop the country, to save the people. [242]William Davis visited Russia after the purge in the late 1950s and sought out the Black Americans who had been living there throughout the murders. Davis encountered a small Black American community and wrote about three of the Negroes which he encountered there. Robert Ross, George Tynes and Robert Robinson. Ross came to Russia in 1927 and Robinson, "had been offered a contract by the Soviet Union to go to that country as a specialist in engineering. He became senior engineer at the first State Ball Bearing Plant in Moscow. In 1934 he was elected to the Moscow City Council where he sat with Stalin, Khrushchev, Molotov, and others. He produced about 27 industrial inventions," for Russia. George Tynes, "a negro soviet citizen, was an expert on farming and the technical director of a game reserve and considered the leading authority on fish and ducks." Lenin tried to address the food shortages by soliciting help from experienced Black agriculturists to teach the Slavic people how to farm. A skill which was badly needed because millions were dying from starvation.

Figure 97 a) Image # 17130("M. Markov, Ksenla Abashidze, (left) a member of the N. Lakoba collective farm, picking maize on the farm with other members of the collective, gelatin silver print, ca. 1935. Print recto.") Maclaren Art exhibitions from Sovfoto-binder of images from Russian history 1936-1957 b) Image #17131 Actor Wayland Rudd taking part in elections December 12th, 1937

Aryan lynch cells began to metastasize throughout the country in direct response to this awakening among Blacks. James Weldon Johnson coined the term Red summer, to refer to the mass insurrection, burning, lynching and destruction of Black communities, across the country. At this time the most influential contributors to the reconstruction, were either dead or severely paralyzed by government surveillance. One of the most flamboyant, Political activist, Casper Holstein 1876-1944 was a successful investor and the pioneer of New York's State lottery. He was kidnapped and ransomed and then arrested for his lottery business, which was considered illegal, but after his death, the State created the first lottery system in the country, and have profited billions. Other prominent Blacks who were the financiers behind the Black resistance were all dying out. Garvey christened his Black Cross Liner in 1923 and started to

[241] The New York Herald-Tribune: "Alleged Red Plot to convert Negroes into Bolshevists." New York, June 28 – (AP)- June 29, 1927 HC
[242] Davis, William How Negroes live in Russia. January 1960 Ebony magazine

carry on regular passenger and freight business between New York, Cuba, Haiti, Colon and Jamaica. Two years later, in 1925 he was arrested, sentenced to five years in prison. His ships were all dismantled, in 1927 and he was deported to Jamaica, and around this same time Lenin died, and then the Bolsheviks were taken over by Josef Stalin, a Georgian.

Stalin's agenda was completely discontinuous to Lenin's. He actually strived to destroy the Bolsheviks from within and to reverse and erase Lenin, like Johnson, Lincoln's vice President reversed much of his work. He began by purging the government of all Lenin's officials and from the onset of Stalin's reign in the 1930s through the end of WWII, over 30 million people were deliberately wiped out. The distinction between the sides during World War II is a lot more complicated than Germany verses the allies. After Lenin died, all of the members of his administration and his military were executed under the leadership of Stalin. This is reminiscent of Thomas Jefferson's silent war or coup d'état, which secretly replaced the Old powers while maintaining the edifice of continuity. Stalin's agenda was to reverse and erase Lenin, like Johnson, Lincoln's vice President reversed much of his work.

[243]"One basic misconception, concerns the moral framework of the war; many Westerners imagine that the war in Europe saw just one evil regime, the third Reich of Adolf Hitler... In reality, the largest combatant power of the war, the Soviet Union of Joseph Stalin... began the war in September 1939 as Hitler's partner in crime." Their rise from the Prussian region, was meant to [244]"stamp out, what Bonaparte and Napoleon III left undone... At this time there was hardly a stone on the continent of Europe which did not speak of the superiority of the past... But Hitler's greatest opponents, the older Prussian aristocracy eventually lost their estates to the "Czechs or the Poles," and their pleas for policy aimed at a return to small kingdoms of chocolate soldiers and picturesque localism," was ignored.

[245]"Stalin by no means agreed with Lenin on all matters, even though he belonged to the Bolshevik faction... As early as the mid-thirties, Stalin began his campaign to exterminate the basic Leninist cadres of the party... but in dealing with such Bolsheviks who were intimates of Lenin, Stalin resorted to the most refined and cynical methods." Lovett-Fort-Whiteman, was a [246]"Black expatriate known to have died in the Stalinist purges." In his early period in the Soviet Union, when he was heading the ANLC, (in the US) he happily travelled back and forth to the United States as he took responsibility for drawing other Blacks to the Soviet Union. But his 1928 return to the Soviet Union proved fateful, for he was never able to leave the country again."

Paul Robeson and W.E. B Dubois were two other Americans who had travelled extensively through Russia during Whiteman's era. Robeson was an international star known for his music and his role as a Moor in Othello. Both he and Dubois were denied reissue of their passports, barred from returning to Russia, and placed under surveillance for communist activity. Robeson once stated that he was only alive because they couldn't catch him. Stalin's process of ridding himself of the Bolshevik leaders coincides with the immigration restrictions placed on Black Americans like Paul Robeson into the USSR. The agenda had clearly changed with the new leadership.

---

[243] Pilecki, Witold Jarek Garlinski The Auschwitz Volunteer: Beyond Bravery Trade select Limited, 2012 pg. XI
[244] Memoirs 1925-1950 George F Kennan An Atlantic Monthly Press Bk 1967 118-121
[245] Medvedev, Roy A. and George Shriver. *Let History Judge: The Origins and Consequences of Stalinism.* Columbia University Press, 1989 15,33
[246] Carew, Joy Gleason Blacks, Reds, and Russians: Sojourners in Search of the Soviet Promise Rutgers University Press, 2010 179

[247] "By the end of 1930, roughly 80 percent of village churches had been closed and among the "disposed Kulaks" were a substantial number of clergymen." [248]Stalin's destruction of the church was only hindered by the mass out cry of the peasants. This was the reason why the Nazis were invited; because Stalin would have lost support from his people in trying to destroy their country. But it is apparent that Hitler simply finished what Stalin had already started and this continuity lends credence to the assertion that these two were connected. This once again is a strategy from the old Thomas Jefferson play book. Jefferson invited the British army to destroy Washington and all the old records, which he then replaced with his own library.

Most Europeans were unaware of the elaborate and historical orchestration behind these mass acts of genocide. But Stalin's ultimate goal was to eliminate as many non-Germanic people, as would be needed to reduce the racial heterogeneity of the country. This was the doctrine of Pan Slavism, that [249] "Russia should take the lead in liberating the Slavic peoples still under Austro-Hungarian and Turkish rule…" They recognized an alarming relationship between Russia's national minorities and their role in the balance of power. [250] "In a country where more than one-half of the population, living in some of its politically most sensitive areas, consisted of peoples other than the dominant Great Russians, this relationship could not fail to be of central importance. As was amply illustrated in the years of crisis following the revolution of 1905, the leaders of the national minorities not only played a prominent role in the movements… but in some cases, were also prepared to secede and even assist Russia's enemies in time of crisis." These leaders were the very Bolsheviks they needed to exterminate.

A Russian survivor of the Soviet purges, Eugenia Ginsburg understood that the Russians were simply eliminating the Moor's from Russia. She echoed the mantra of Friedrich von Schiller from Fiesco's Conspiracy at Genoa. [251]"the Moor has done his job, the Moor can go." The term Moor is obsolete today, but in the past century, a Moor was described as a [252] "native of the northern coast of Africa, called by the Romans from the color of the people, Mauritania, the country of dark complexioned people. According to the Oxford Universal dictionary reprinted with Addenda in 1955: The Moors were supposed to be mostly Black or very swarthy and hence the word has often been used for 'negro.' Once the names are changed, then the information which would have been connected to these words are altered or erased. This explains how people were erased physically by the genocides but were also robbed of their historic identity and accomplishments to bolster this propaganda.

George Orwell's story '1984,' published in 1949 during the end of WWII, was a prophecy of what Orwell anticipated of the world by "1984." [253]"The eleventh edition is the definitive edition… We're getting the language into its final shape, the shape it's going to have when nobody speaks anything else…You think I dare say that our chief job is inventing new words. But not a bit of it! We're destroying words-scores of them, hundreds of them, every day. The eleventh edition won't contain a single word that will become obsolete before the year 2050." So the names like the people they represented would be

[247] ibid 15 &230

[248] Viola, Lynne. Peasant Rebels Under Stalin: Collectivization and the Culture of Peasant Resistance. Oxford University Press, Jan 28, 1999 40

[249]Lederer, Ivo J. Russian Foreign *Policy Essays in Historical Perspective.* New Haven and London University Press. (as represented by R.A. Fadeev's Opinion on the Eastern Question and N. Ia. Danilevskii's Russia and Europe published in 1869) pg. 26 Russian Foreign Policy.

[250] Ibid… 30

[251]Ginzburg, Eugenia *Journey into the Whirlwind* Houghton Mifflin Harcourt, Nov 4, 2002 139

[252] Webster, Noah. *A Dictionary of the English Language: in Two Volumes*, Volume 2, Black and Young, 1832

[253] Orwell, George *1984* Signet classic by New American Library a division of Penguin Group. 51

redacted from all records. The editors of Webster's New International dictionary, (New for 1914) said that the New dictionary "was entirely remade: the previous material sifted and rearranged; the definitions treated with nicer discrimination. In short, the New international is essentially a new book." "At present a difficulty exists for lexicographers in the fact that advocacy of proposed changes is very active. A radical and rapidly progressive change is being urged by an organized propaganda, but the popular response, by actual practice, is as yet slight." The depths of "organization," involved in this propaganda cannot be overstated. "New" dictionaries and historic analysis, altered definitions and information to remove the ethnographic markers, and so the names like the people they were exterminating like Creoles, Moors, Jews and Zinganies were also erased or distorted. So words like Zingani and Circassian have been eliminated, but the most pervasive have been redefined so that an "Ottoman" now represents a foot stool while the Moor represents "dirt," to be tread under foot or something held in place or fastened.

[254] "In an effort to preserve the cultural and historical memorials of the Russian people connected with the life and creations of the gifted Russian poet and genius, Alexander Pushkin, the Bolsheivks on 17th March 1922, declared the poet's estate, a state reservation..." Lenin's preservation of Pushkin's archives and care to protect the institution of the church from any state interference is important to determine a disconnection between the Soviet regime which later suppressed movement and censored the press among other subversive actions.

A 2004 travel guide noted that, [255]By the time of the purges, Russia had lost over a third of its almost 100,000 churches

Figure 98 A large variety of items for sale at the popular weekend Izmailovsky Flea Market, in Russia including discarded old "Black," religious icons. Nordbye Travel guide 197

and monasteries. Churches were turned into swimming pools, ice skating rinks and atheist museums. Although Stalin assumed power, his government could not desecrate their own monuments, (just as Thomas Jefferson could not burn the archives of his own government). What the Tsars attempted to suppress had been memorialized by Lenin; so, the Germans were commissioned to finish the job. [256] "In July 1941, the Hitlerite's forced their way into the Pushkin reservation and made themselves at home there… The Hitlerite's destroyed and annihilated the cultural-historic monuments of the Russian people connected with the life and work of the great Russian poet, Alexander Pushkin." [257] Their Nazi conspirators destroyed 1,670 Greek Orthodox Churches, 237 Roman Catholic Churches, 67 Chapels, 427 museums and many thousands of residential buildings: they removed 10,000 works of art: Many books and records were burned in an attempt to erase every indication of a Black presence from Russia. The Nazis were in the twentieth century what ISIL is to this century. They pulled off the greatest heist in

---

[254] International Military Tribunal, Nuremberg. "Document # USSR-40 (Exhibit # USSR 40)" 1946 75-76
[255] Nordbye, Masha. *Moscow, St Petersburg and the Golden Ring* 2nd Edition 243-244
[256] Ibid
[257] Nazi Conspiracy and Aggression, (Volume 4) United States. Office of Chief of Counsel for the Prosecution of Axis Criminality U.S. Government Printing Office, 1946

world history. They made off with more than gold and property, they stole entire countries and the history of those they executed.

When comparing the accounts of, Polish survivor Witold Pilecki, who witnessed the murder of the Bolsheviks at Auschwitz to Russian survivor Eugenia Ginsburg, who experienced the purging of the Soviet top-ranking administration, the conspiracy is evident. [258] Ginsburg says that, "in the autumn of 1935 the authorities began to arrest everyone who had ever been connected with the opposition." She and many others spent several years in prison. "Hardly anyone at the time realized that purges of this sort were carried out strictly in accordance with a prearranged plan…"

Figure 99 a) Corpses were stripped of their uniforms and jewelry prior to execution. Then the murderers traded places with their victims. b) Bags of Gold loot stored in Merkers 1943-1946 by Donald Ornitz

Like everyone else among the intelligentsia, Ginsburg was shocked by the atrocities which seemed to lay in-discriminant claim to the lives of her colleagues. [259]"We could not understand this at the time. Later we were to learn that the purge of the NKVD itself had already begun. The Moor has done his duty-the Moor can go." Ginsburg never saw where they were being taken to, but Stalin replaced all top-ranking officials and Bolshevik officers with their subordinates. He then sent these officials to be killed by the Nazis. According to Pilecki, these officials were being taken to Auschwitz; where he witnessed [260] "the first Bolshevik prisoners… were brought in and after seven hundred of them were locked so tightly in a room that none could sit, the room was sealed, and a group of German soldiers threw in a few gas canisters and observed the effects. "They must have been Bolshevik senior ranks judging by the uniforms." It is clear that the Nazi killings of the Bolsheviks was organized by Stalin.

The conspiracy only becomes apparent when these accounts are examined together. Viktor Suvorov, [261]"a pseudonym for a former soviet staff officer now resident in the West," said [262]"the Communist and Nazi parties did attempt a joint takeover in Germany in 1923. Communist propaganda wants us to believe that there was no conspiracy between communists and Nazis; but this attempt was undertaken in the fall of 1923 when Lenin no longer participated in the leadership. Stalin earmarked tremendous funds to support the German revolution, and a decision was made to support the effort without limits. The first time that

[258] Ginzburg, Eugenia. *Journey into the Whirlwind* Houghton Mifflin Harcourt, Nov 4, 2002 pg. 17
[259] Ibid. 139
[260] Pilecki, Witold Jarek Garlinski *The Auschwitz Volunteer: Beyond Bravery* Trade select Limited, 2012 p.131
[261] B. Peake Hayden, *The Intelligence Officer's Bookshelf Studies in Intelligence* Vol.53, No 3 compiled and reviewed by CIA (Extracts, September 2010) 51
[262] Suvorov, Viktor. *The Chief Culprit: Stalin's Grand Design to Start World War II*. Naval Institute Press, Feb 18, 2013

Stalin spoke before the military graduates, was right when the great purge was secretly being planned. But Stalin had in mind nothing less than the complete extermination of almost all of the communist hierarchy, state, party, military, technical, scientific, cultural, and all others. Stalin planned almost a complete transformation of the leading layer of the country. Almost everyone who listened to Stalin's speech in 1935 in two years landed in torture chambers and execution cellars."

Then like the Jeffersonian take-over of America, the German-Russian alliance produced their own version of the events, so that, [263]"all Russian history, but particularly that of modern times, was completely dominated by the party's ideological organs, which tailored the facts and interpretations to suit the current party line... Soviet historical literature had little to do with what actually happened but instead reflected what the establishment wanted people to believe." Unfortunately, this is not restricted to Russian history. Pipes also argues that this revisionist perspective has permeated US, British and German scholarship and "during the past three decades there has occurred a *convergence* of approaches between Soviet and Western historiography. He believes that, Historians have also played a major role in forging a seamless unity between the immutable power of the past and the irresistible force of this ideology.

This has fostered the illusion of a master race and its motive to eliminate inferior ethnicities within their domain. This claim of Aryan supremacy is deeply rooted, not only in the claim to European territory as the native people, but as the chief architects of this civilization. This disguises the diversity and heterogeneity which pervaded all European society before WWII, and serves to erase the contributions of others. To promote this perspective the information like the many millions of victims of genocide, has suffered from extreme redaction or in most cases complete obliteration.

A closer examination into the pre-genocidal era after WWI highlights a decline in birth rates. [264] "Birth rates had notably diminished in all of the four leading European Nations-Great Britain, Germany, France and Italy. Italy was aroused by figures indicating that the births for the first ten months of the year 1927 were about 100,000 fewer than for the same period of the previous year. The rate of the decrease is slow, but it is estimated that if the present trend continues there will be no more births than deaths twenty years hence." Newspapers warned that they might one-day face depopulation if this tendency continued. This debunks the argument that the war was started, because the Germans needed territory for the growing population. This decline in birth rate, may have disproportionally affected the Germanic population verses the others, who were said to account for a substantial portion of the population.

The root cause of the genocides in 20th century Russian and German society can be directly attributed to a declining birth rate among the Aryans, in the face of a large population of many 'others' who occupied very crucial territory, coupled with the threat that these citizens were inviting more Blacks in an attempt to form a unified force against the New World capitalist and imperial structures. The US government terrorized Blacks, labeled them dreaded un-American communists, and confiscated their passports, while Hitler, Stalin and Roosevelt took turns, to grace the cover of the Times magazine, as 'Man of the Year.'

The objective is clear, the *Great Russians* needed to take control of the remaining regions under Ottoman control from the Black Sea to the Mediterranean and as far south as the Holy Land. [265]"For hundreds of years before the first World War, Palestine belonged to Turkey and at the end of the war, the League of Nations placed the government in the hands of the British and there **is** a plan... (in 1930,

---

[263] Pipes, Richard Three "Whys" of the Russian Revolution. Vintage Books Division of Random House New York. 1995 6,8,23
[264] Callender, Harold. "Fall in Birth Rates Aids Peace of Europe." New York Times. March 18, 1928
[265] Wallace Atwood and Helen Goss Thomas 1930 Nations Beyond the Seas pg. 72

fifteen years before WWII) to make Palestine a new homeland for the Jews." This plan was not a whim of war, but had long been devised as part of the New World Order of the gilded era and was already in place by the mid-19th century. There was no way to achieve total autonomy in Europe without the control of the most significant boarders for shipping and international trade. They needed to take over the regions under Ottoman control, from the Riga line to the Black Sea, the Mediterranean and as far south as the Holy Land. [266]"Hence the order for the Jews to quit the Russian empire, within a given period, who amount to perhaps 2,000,000 in that region. Thus, to re-instate them in the land of Canaan, to become as a Russian province for that empire." So, the Aryans killed off the Jews and many posed as refugees to take over the crucial region of the Middle East.

This plan called for "effective occupation," to achieve Germanization and Russification and clear the land of the diverse population, and this plan was at least a century old. It had its origins from the gilded era and Jefferson's successors. [267]"When the Eastern border of Prussia was consolidated as German territory in 1871, Polish nationalism intensified, and the Prussian settlement commission sent in more Germans. In the thirty years of its existence (1886 to 1916) the commission transplanted some 130,000 Aryans." This mass immigration into the Middle East, is the cause of decades of subsequent wars for territory there; but this scheme was no longer viable due to the declining population of Aryans in Prussia, as well as fierce resistance by the Moors. Thus the [268]outright extermination of people all over the world. [269]They would now have Prussia, Austria and Italy, as they already had England, France, America and Spain. The great Russians succeeded in much more than Russifying, Russia and Germanizing Germany, as a bonus they also managed to take occupation of the Holy Land, and Russian born Chaim Weizmann president of the World Zionist Organization worked to bring Aryan Jews to Palestine to build up a Jewish National home. This idea of transplanting and gradually replacing was a systematic process of colonization, not a result of war, but its objective. Then the allied invasion of North Africa from Morocco and Algeria called *Operation Torch* in 1942 brought Vichy France under full axis occupation. It became a purely Aryan occupation in the fall of 1943 after Italy's surrender.

In 1943 Tunis the last remaining Axis position in North Africa fell." Then a large number of Aryans moved into North Africa. As in Russia and American history, Operation Torch was always meant to destroy any history or evidence of the people that they were trying to erase. These forces were not able to plow through Africa with a torch, because their actions would have been obvious. To penetrate Wakanda, or Timbuctoo and destroy their vast library of evidence would require some skill. In 1988 a site was built to gather the manuscripts into one central location, and then the site was then added to the UNESCO World heritage list. Then in 2012 French forces occupied the region, and in 2015 many of the archives were torched.

---

[266] Dow, Lorenzo. The Dealings of God, Man and the Devil: As Exemplified in the Life, Experience, and Travels of Lorenzo Dow, in a Period of Over Half a Century, Volume 2 Nafia & Cornish, 1850. 178

[267] Dwork, Deborah and Robert Jan Pelt. Auschwitz, 1270 to the Present. W. W. Norton & Company, 1996 48-49

[268] An in-depth analysis of the connection between the genocides which took place from Armenia in 1815 to Rwanda in 1992 is covered in Our Story.

[269] The United States in 1800 by Henry Adams, Man and Society Vol. 6 Gateway to great Books 1963 pg.344

Figure 100 North-African soldiers, 1917. By Jean-Baptiste Tournassoud

In Hawaii, the natives were forced off their land and in 1900, Sanford B. Dole, was sworn in as the *first* governor. The U.S begun to impose education systems which outlawed the teaching of native languages. Then the subtle genocide of Hawaiians as foreigners, like Dole, quickly came in to take over most of the land which they continue to possess to this day. This pattern was followed in almost every country that the new European and American rulers entered. In 1937, Blacks were forced out of Western Hispaniola into what became Haiti. A barren strip of land which was once used to extract timber. Then the Dominican Republic was created with a new Aryanized group placed in power. The Herero Genocide took place in the German held region of Namibia shortly after. German general Lothar von Trotha, drove the Namibians into the desert, where it is estimated that more than 80,000 people died. Trotha warned that, "within the German boundaries, every Herero, whether armed or unarmed, will be shot."

Figure 101 a) Herero fugitives b)People of India Left to starve and asked to pose for a photos c) Vultures devour dead carcasses in India.

Then these people now wandering vagabonds, become the object of scorn and ridicule. [270]Death in several forms—massacre, starvation, exhaustion. In 1945 millions were isolated in India and left to starve. [271]In the 1970's millions of Vietnamese living among a majority of Cambodians, were wiped out. In Bosnia and Herzegovina almost 100,000 people were killed between 1992–1995. This was a process of

---

[270] Morgenthau, Henry (1918). Ambassador Morgenthau's Story. Garden City, New York: Doubleday.

[271] Ebony magazine pg 167 August 1970 issue.

programmed global genocide, but it was too vast to be accomplished within one generation. The subsequent genocides may all be connected. In 1994 after German and Belgium forces evacuated Rwanda it is estimated that nearly a million people were massacred. Reports say that the Germans were playing one side against another and they were the invisible hand behind the civil discord. [272]In the early twenties in Chicago, drive by shootings were the habitual terror tactics of the Nazis. Later guns were dropped off into depressed neighborhoods and a century of civil war still continues there.

Today many are unaware of the depths of destruction which have taken place. How easily they have been systematically erased from one story to another and what could not be claimed, given to others. Even in this generation, terms like 'Negro,' are being substituted for African American and *African* history is now on schedule to be rewritten. So that our descendants will one day ask, [273]"How did Africa get so Black?" Webster noted, that the destructive tendencies of the Aryans could be overcome with the gospel, but Jefferson and succeeding generations choose to bury this message. Instead a technologically advanced Barbarian has evolved.

Figure 102 "Dread & Terrible," twentieth Century Ethiopian Soldiers. Ethiopia was the only country in Africa to withstand invasion.

The Barbarian [274]*"need not appear in bearskin with a club in hand. He may wear a brooks Brothers suit. In fact, beneath the academic gown, there may lurk a child of the wilderness, in the high tradition of civility... engaged in the construction of philosophy to put an end to all philosophy. This is perennially, the work of the Barbarian, to undermine rational standards of judgement, to corrupt the inherited intuitive wisdom by which people have always lived, and to do this not by spreading new beliefs, but by creating a climate of doubt and bewilderment in which clarity about the larger aims of life is dimmed and the self-confidence of the people destroyed, leaving the impotent nihilism of the "generation of the third eye,' now presently appearing on our university campuses.*

---

[272] Women's Home Missions of the Methodist Episcopal Church Women's Home Missionary Society of the Methodist Church vl 37-38 1920vl 37-38 1920 pg10

[273] Best-selling book, "Guns Germs and Steel" the author asks in the twenty-first century, "How did Africa get so Black?" He proceeds to provide a contemporary explanation, for what he considers a modern perception.

[274] We hold these truths, Catholic Reflections on the American proposition. John Courtney Murray, S.J Sheed and Ward INC 1960 pg.12-24

The Spiritual Force
An Obstacle to the New World

The plan for a global take over, was a revolution so conspicuous and so meticulously guarded that it has taken nearly two centuries to put all the pieces together.

[275]"Of course, in the pages of official history, we shall find no explanation of this sudden recurrence of the revolutionary epidemic, which is once more conveniently ascribed to the time-honored theory of contagious popular enthusiasm for liberty. Thus, the Cambridge Modern History, describing the revolution in Germany, observes: "The Grand Duchy of Baden was the natural starting-place for the revolutionary movement, which, once set on foot, seemed to progress almost automatically from State to State and town to town." Precisely; but we are given no hint as to the mechanism which produced this automatic action all over Europe. The business of the official historian is not to inquire into causes but to present the sequence of events in a manner unintelligible to the philosopher but satisfying to the uninquiring mind of the general public. That the European Revolution of 1848 was the result of masonic organization cannot, however, be doubted by anyone who takes trouble to dig below the surface."

It is generally understood among scholars, that any mention of a secret society or illuminati, would be professional suicide. The historian who seeks to be taken seriously must follow the pattern already outlined, the journalist must also report from that angle. Thus we are all warped into this lie. [276]"The crisis of today is then no development of modern times, but a mere continuation of the immense movement that began in the middle of the eighteenth century. In a word, it is all one and the same revolution."

Figure 103 Man posing on top and in front of a mountain of dry bones, from the bison slaughtered to starve out the Blacks.

In the beginning of this global takeover, British and American forces, used the already established networks of the church to enter into the countries they would later invade, to take over. In the early nineteenth century, the Aryan realized that the gospel he was spreading around the world, predicted his defeat. The growing awareness that the Aryan, was perpetually trapped within an ideological framework, which guaranteed his defeat, led to the formation of the Eugenics theology. This modern-day lens empowered New World leaders, to portray the world

---

[275] Webster, Nesta World Revolution The Plot Against Civilization, Small, Maynard & Co Publishers Boston pg.
[276] Ibid: World Revolution viii

94

through a dramatically new set of ideas; which [277]"grew out of the theory of evolution, to change the course of men's thinking. Before these ideas burst upon the horizon, it was for example, generally held that the world had been created in precisely the year 4004 BC." This changed the story entirely, so that the actions of the aggressor could now be framed as acts of the fittest against the unfit. Herbert Spencer worked (during the Nadir period) from 1860 to 1903 on a new synthesis of knowledge, which brought this scientific theory of evolution to the social arena. [278]"The evils of child labor, poverty, unemployment, and industrial warfare which were rampant in Western Europe and America, were justified, because they were the means to that perfect society. Every social and industrial violence, every outrage caused by competition, was given an aura of destined good in the philosophy of social Darwinism. A central figure in this struggle was the *superman*. In his ruthless quest for power, this giant among men would help along the selection of the fittest by crushing the weak and helpless."

Once the new social order was established, all that remained was the actual extermination of the weak and helpless. There was no opportunity to surrender, those who were already defeated, were never free. The war could never end until they were eliminated. America passed laws for the prohibition of alcohol and this retarded the Caribbean islands which provided the sugar to produce spirits and molasses. Prohibition was especially crippling for Black American Distillers. When their factories succumbed to repeated arsons, or prohibition, speculators bought them out at pennies on the dollar. Neares or Nathan Green, from Moore County Tennessee became Jack Daniels whiskey and the state's most prosperous Tavern, Black Bob's Tavern, run by Bob Renfroe as early as 1792, vanished without a trace. These are a few examples of how the industries and traditions held by Blacks, were soon overtaken by Whites. [279]Then the War Prohibition Bureau, collected millions of dollars in fines and the confiscation of property, typically biased against Blacks. Before the revolution, [280]salt was the only preservative, it had to be shipped at great price from the West Indies. But the West Indies, was simply a stop from the shipping point of North Africa. After North Africa was invaded, the map was redrawn, and the African and Caribbean middle men were excluded. Gold and other products which the Africans once monopolized reduced in value, from its discovery in America, while products like ivory were outlawed. Then the crippled African nations were invaded, plundered and forced to pay tribute to the looters, who laundered their loot into global banks. Then they returned to these defeated nations to loan them from their loot, and were now in the position to dictate to these countries the terms of their government. Countries like Nicaragua, Cuba, Haiti and Guyana among many others were simply excluded from the global economy and left to ruin. Any country, which begun to make progress and show signs of breaking out of the cycle of interdependence, like Libya, Cuba, Grenada, Nicaragua and Venezuela would then develop instability from the unseen infiltration of these Aryan instigators, who would lead these nations on to a path of their own undoing.

Overnight masas became slaves, naked and barefoot once again. The rise of the Aryans, cannot be disentangled from a legacy of barbaric and heinous piracy. The pirates then established

[277] Walcutt, Charles: Jack London University of Minnesota pamphlets on American writers no. 57 page 6 1966 North Central publishing co St. Paul
[278] Ibid
[279] The war on prohibition and the rise of the American State. Lisa MC
[280] Alistair Cooke's America, Alfred A knopf INc, New York 1973 Borzoi Books p158

themselves as the legal and moral authority and proceeded to subjugate and perpetually terrorize the remnant of Blacks around the world. With new international maritime laws enacted, the situations faced by Africans worldwide was never communicated. Blacks were marked for extinction, and the remnant would have been sent to reserves, like some of the natives of America and Australia. At home and abroad segregation and racism ensured that the lines of power and poverty could never be crossed; so that what was taken with arms could now be retained by diplomacy.

Figure 104 Battle of Isandlwana by Charles Edwin Fripp (1854–1906)
This image is represents the aim of psychological conditioning which has successfully reduced Black people to caricatures of Supremacist amusement. It is also an example of Twain's concept of "Trading Places." Notice that the Blacks are now naked and the Whites are fully clothed

The Christian ideology, was the most significant obstacle to the [281]White race from Europe overrunning and colonizing… It was the growing sentiment which was increasingly influencing public opinion, in Europe more especially, which forbid the White man to do evil that good may come; namely, to displace by force of arms pre-existing races in order that the White man may take the land they occupy for his own use;" so the Aryans began a campaign to de-Christianize the world. Their victory in the stokes trial, essentially outlawed teaching the creation world view. But the ultimate objective was to supplement the moral and ethical frame work of the Christian doctrine, with the new Aryan theology of a master race, which had taken "a great leap forward," from the African abyss and evolved into an advanced race of men. This agenda was adopted through institutions of higher learning and trickled down to the masses as the new "intellectually" advanced theory. Hitler declared that if he controlled the text books he would control the state." Education once again, became the open door to an underground revolution. The new secular theology facilitated a widespread climate of doubt and separated the educated from the ignorant as seculars from Christians. The principles of faith became archaic symbols of primitive man, while the new secular direction was associated with new world advancement.

The teaching of creation, was then replaced with the new theology of evolution and social Darwinism. [282] They believed that if they could banish Christianity from France, they would then be able to reason more easily with others… because, she had been the greatest most attached to the Holy See, and the most fertile in apostles of the bible.... so, anti-Christian sects (began) conspiring with the object of de-Christianizing the world, commenced with France.

---

[281] Larned, Josephus Nelson and Alan Campbell Riley *History for Ready Reference: From the Best Historians, Biographers, and Specialists; Their Own Words in a Complete System of History*. C.A. Nichols Company, 1910.

[282]Special to the New York Times. Lucon Assails New Law: Says Attempts to De Christianize the world has begun in France. New York Times Feb 4, 1925

Despite these ambitious efforts, White supremacy was continuously defeated by the Christian ideology, of universal brotherhood. This religious and moral compass helped to mobilize and galvanize all grievances, into national campaigns for civil rights. The Christian doctrine was the most significant force which White supremacists fought against, because it confounded their efforts into biblical narratives like David verses Goliath. This always had the result of casting the supremacist agenda, as analogous to that of the antagonist of scripture "the devil." In this socio-cultural milieu, the Aryans consistently personified the dubious characteristics of the evil menace to society; making; the ideological sides clear. On the one end was the cunning and powerful master of deception, the oppressor, skillful liar, thief and destroyer, whose every attack seemed to propagate this philosophy and strengthen the vigilance of the meek, oppressed and lowly. Every scheme and every stone made them hopeful, justified and reinforced their faith that the battle would be won.

Figure 105 Mural of Alexander Henson planting the American flag at North Pole, by Austin Mecklem, at the Recorder of Deeds building, built in 1943. 515 D St., NW, Washington, D.C.

In 1924 Mathew Henson was the first American to reach the North Pole, but Peary a White man received the medal of honor, with no mention of Henson. This deliberate and prevalent omission of Blacks from the narrative, prompted Carter Woodson to create a separate record keeping for Black history month, but this effort only aided the usurpers in cementing their story. Black history was reduced to a segregated tale of otherness, a collection of facts disconnected from the new White American version.

James Weldon Johnson (1871–1938) CEO of the NAACP from 1920 to 1930, decided that Blacks needed a new national anthem, to lift their spirits and keep them treading along through their traumatic existence. He is best remembered for his composition of the Negro National Anthem"— "Lift Every Voice and Sing" which was written as a poem in 1899. Amidst the obscurity of the 'Nadir' and 'Gilded' Ages, and extreme violence, faith embodied the Negro spiritual. Faith provided a vision for the future and faith in this future guided Americans on a trajectory to an unrealized path forward. A place in time which they were certain existed. It was a heaven which awaited their descendants and the force of this vision clearly motivated our ancestors to work together to see it realized.

But as the old saying goes, if you can't beat them, join them. The effort to deChristianize Europe failed; because most Europeans rejected the Aryan agenda, so that Hitler was forced to embrace it. The Nazi's declared themselves the chosen and found biblical justification for their actions. But the general agenda to move away from the Judeo-Christian philosophy remained the vision for the future generation. The unyielding efforts to distort information and control the narrative, could not be achieved as subtly, in the twentieth century, as it had been in the gilded age. Television and other technological advances to communication, meant more people had greater access to information. This meant that the age of alternative facts, met with instant fact checkers. The failure of their hidden strategies led the Klan to revert to its former acts of overt terrorism. They became bolder and more aggressive against Blacks. But the beat was changing, and Americans began to move to it. Chuck Berry gave birth to a new genre of music which altered the dreary beat of the Blues, by adding some rhythm. A genre that would be called Rhythm and Blues and eventually Rock and Roll. After the stokes trial and the national agenda to "de-Christianize," the nation failed to bring about the changes that were necessary to perpetuate discrimination, this led to a great deal of agitation on the part of supremacists.[283]"As a result of the failure of their strategies, the Klan began to rise again. The US justice department reported that, from 1954 to 1965, the Klan was responsible for 70 bombings in Georgia and Mississippi 30 Black churches in Mississippi and 50 in Montgomery, Alabama.

Although the hidden agenda to relegate Blacks to the bottom of the social ladder, was being rejected by many Americans, Blacks and Whites; it was everywhere even [284]imbedded within the criminal justice system; which represents one of the most overt forms of organized sabotage. The system restricted the freedom of Blacks and diminished their political influence. Although, many of those who rose up to resist, the organized and government backed tactics, were punished, faith continued to fuel works and tireless militancy. Civil Rights activists who were often church leaders like, Martin Luther King, and Senator Adam Clayton Powell, Jr. (1908 – 1972) mobilized their congregations to protest the injustice which was beginning to escalate. King explained that he left Atlanta to fight in Birmingham Alabama, because injustice was there; and he was simply [285]"following the examples of the prophets of the bible who left their little villages to carry "thus saith the lord" far beyond the boundaries of their hometowns."

Figure 106 a)Adam Clayton Powell, guarded by his supporters. B) John Fitzgerald Kennedy

Senator Powell was a Baptist pastor and the first African-American elected from New York to Congress since the end of the Nadir. Powell represented Harlem, in the US House of Representatives from (1945–71), during his tenure, John *Fitzgerald* Kennedy, became president from 1961-1963 and other more well-known leaders like supreme court justice, Thurgood Marshall, Martin Luther King and Malcomb X were all resisting the efforts of the Aryans, and a more globalized understanding of what was happening begun to take shape. Kennedy, an Irish Catholic was assassinated in 1963.

---

[283] The Connecticut Education Association, The council on interracial Books for children and the National Education Association. *Violence, The Klu Klux Klan and the struggle for equality. An informational and instructional kit.* May 1981 pg. 16

[284] Alexander, Michelle *The New Jim Crow: Mass Incarceration in the Age of Colorblindness.* The New Press, Dec 13, 2013

[285] King, Dr. Martin Luther Jr. Why We Can't Wait Beacon Press, Jan 11, 2011

High-Level Talk In Low Tones: In Cuba for conferences with President Manuel Urretia and army chief Fidel Castro (r.) as U. S. indignation mounted against executions Congressman Adam Powell confers with rebel leader or fair trials for "war criminals" during Havana reception

Figure 107 Senator Clayton Powell and Fidel Castro in Havana

Suddenly, the plight of Steve Biko and Mandela, in South Africa, Castro in Cuba, Foneseca in Nicaragua and others around the globe, revealed the hypocrisy of the New World leaders. All except for Mandela and Castro met with untimely deaths. In June 1966 in Lowndes County, Alabama, Stokely Carmichael, took the mantel through the Student Non-violent Coordinating Committee, (SNCC) to promote a radical militant stand against White supremacists. In a speech which advocated Black assertiveness, he coined the term "Black Power." SNCC mobilized the Alabama County where 80% of the population were Black into a political force which took control of their government through the creation of a political party. Despite the theological diversity among Black congregations, most black churches prioritized issues of social justice. Dr. Huey Newton and Bobby Seale in response to Carmichael's appeal, began the Black Panthers Party, for Self-Defense and organized some of their programs in Oakland's Saint Augustine Episcopal Church. The CRIPS or Community Revolution In Progress, were labelled as a violent gang, but rose originally in response to the terrorism of White supremacists.

Figure 108 Black Panther's took their guns to congress

The church was another institution which was affected by subtle legislation to weaken its social authority. The church today, though grounded in the [286]African American emotional and musical heritage, is now led by pastors with college and advanced degrees and are located in suburbs inaccessible by public transportation. Leaders now appeal to middle class Blacks, who also increasingly believed that personal autonomy, was the best counter to racism, and that those who accepted personal responsibility for their actions would reap God's reward." This underscores the ideological disconnect even among the leadership of these churches and the conditions of the people which they represent. It also demonstrates how the ideology of the White

---

[286] White, Deborah G., Mia Bay, and Waldo E. Martin. *Freedom on My Mind: A History of African Americans, with Documents.* Vol. 2. Bedford, 2013. 788-789

supremacists, have permeated the Christian doctrine, so that pastors now preach a doctrine of self-help and self-empowerment which negates the societal obstacles which persist against their flock. This growing chasm within the church and its leadership, is the laying of a foundation for the defeat of African American development. This is precisely the objective of the Aryan, to illustrate his power in the subjugation of the weak.

[287]"Most Christians have little knowledge of many of the most powerful voices in the rich prophetic tradition in American Christianity. This prophetic Christianity is the ecumenical force for good, and if we are to revitalize the democratic energies of the country, we must reassert the vital legitimacy of this prophetic Christianity." By the end of the sixties many of the laws which legalized segregation and discrimination were banned. During the civil rights movement of the 1960s, there was a desperate attempt to reverse the Aryan frame of reference, and a major emphasis was placed on a reinterpretation in world history. The National Council for the Social Studies, advised that this reinterpretation should include "ethno-history, which is essential to tie the varied ethnic rivulets into the mainstream of human history." This was because of the extent to which historical scholarship was engaged in rewriting history and as a result, "the gap widens between dependable knowledge and what is taught." (Foreword VII) The council hypothesized that the eventual production of balanced world histories would contribute to political stability; and warned that if impartial scholars do not reconstruct these histories scientifically, then "partisans will fabricate faulty histories or create modern myths." The council's request for more ethno-graphically accurate historiography were ignored. "One particular concern was the accelerating pace of transformation of the so-called archaic or primitive peoples, who have long been the subject of Anthropological investigation." This was a concern because, historians could not continue to relate history from the vantage point of a perpetually inferior, captive trying to achieve equality. This is the final revolution, marked by the attempt of the Trump regime, to usurp American democracy. This regime also makes the ideas of this book much more comprehensible. Because without the blatant distortions, of the president, it would be impossible to believe that Jefferson simply created a new and fabricated reality. The danger, is that in about a half century, a historian seeking clarity on America in 2017, may depend solely on the president's words. They would find a man boldly claiming to have inherited a mess and pointing out problems in the face of sky rocketing stock markets, rising employment levels, and home values and almost every facet of American civilization restored to never before greatness. While America has been allied with the European Union, Trump, also like Jefferson chose a new and secret ally. One who has proven to be quite efficient at destroying nations. But unlike Jefferson, Trump and his cast of millionaires represent the dying Federalists, who sought to remedy their demise by removing the millions of Americans who have taken refuge here. Most are Americans, because before the mass relocation of Europeans to the Western Hemisphere, America was inhabited by people who moved freely. These people were then given boundaries, by the ancestors of those who now seek to evict them.

---

[287] West Cornel, *Democracy Matters Winning the Fight Against Imperialism*. The Penguin Press New York 2004

100

But the beat has changed once again, from the Blues to R and B, then to Hip-Hop and Rap. The lyrics are more assertive, militant and revolutionary. Artists claimed that [288]"the clock was ticking we were just counting hours," we were just [289]"on the pulse of morning, and we could see in the distance our long way home," where there would be [290]"glory; but the war is not over victory is not yet won." The pattern of the revolutions in world history, indicates that this generation is in the midst of a new revolution. The major difference between this revolution and those which have preceded it, is that the historic instigators, with the reputation of destroying governments, are now the ones with the political power, wealth and control; and the poor, tired and weak masses are no longer *White*. Thus, for Aryans and White supremacists, this war is an act of self-destruction.

There is [291]"a new cockade, which will go around the world as a symbol of an institution, both civic and military, which must triumph over the antiquated tactics of Europe, because it will leave the autocrat governments only the choice between being beaten by eternal powers if they do not imitate it, or overthrown if they do," because history has proven that destiny manifests to preserve the meek against the proud. Now that the pen has replaced the sword, consider this book, the victory, because we will now write our own story; and when the fog from the smoke of this revolution clears up, know without a doubt that [292]"We gonna be alright."

The sun is rising again, and with it a new period of enlightenment; but soon there will be [293]neither sun nor moon. The American empire, and empires in general will not continue as in the past. Our story will not be one of racial alignment, Americans will be the rock which anchors the symbol of global democracy, they will reject bigotry and work to build a new world and a more perfect union than ever before. The responsibility is largely on the part of the Black community, not to remain confined to the cultural perceptions which have chained us. Now that the Guinee is out of the bottle, the true magic will be a forging of a New American identity. One which will blend all of our voices together, so that we can sing a new song.

---

[288] Kanye West "Power"
[289] Maya Angelo[289] John Legend and Common, Oscar winning song "Glory". [289] Lafayette[289] Kendrick Lamar, "Alright."
[290] Revelation 21:23

Bibliography

1984: Orwell, George Signet classic: New American Library a division of Penguin Group.

A Collection of Voyages and Travels, Volume 2 Awnsham Churchill Asian Educational Services, 1732

A Description of the Western Islands of Scotland: Containing a Full Account of Their Situation, Extent, Soils, Products, Harbors, Bays... With a New Map of the Whole, ... To which is Added a Brief Description of the Isles of Orkney, and Schetland written By, Martin Martin and published by Andrew Bell, at the Cross-Keys and Bible, in Cornhill, near Stocks-Market., 1703

A Dictionary of the English Language: Compiled for the Use of Common Schools in the United States, Webster, Noah George Goodwin, 1817

A Dictionary of the English Language: in Two Volumes, Volume 2, by Webster, Noah. Black and Young, 1832

A Different Vision of African American Economic Thought. Thomas D Boston Psychology Press 1997

A Geneology of South Worths by Samuel Gil

A Handbook of the Swahili Language, as Spoken at Zanzibar. 3d ed. London: Society for Promoting Christian Knowledge, Steere, Edward, and A. C. Madan. 1884.

A History of Architecture in the Americas, Cardinal-Pett, Clare Routledge, 2015

A History of German Literature 6th Edition by J. G Robertson, published by William Blackwood and sons LTD Edinburg and London. 1949

A History of Western Society from antiquity to the enlightenment. Mckay, John, Hill and Buckler, Sixth edition. Houghton Miffin Company 1999

Aleksandr Sergeyevich Pushkin. (2016) Encyclopædia Britannica. Retrieved April, 19 2016 at 5:16pm from http://www.britannica.com/biography/Aleksandr-Sergeyevich-Pushkin

Alistair Cooke's America, Alfred A knopf INc, New York 1973 Borzoi Books p193

American Heritage book of Presidents and famous Americans by AH Publishing Co. 1967

American State papers, Documents, Legislative and Executive of the Congress of the United States

A Modest Proposal for Preventing the Children of Ireland from Being a Burden on their Parents and Country. Swift, Jonathan, Man and society Vol. 7 Gateway to great Books 1963

An Account of the Great Plague of London in the Year 1665: Now First Printed from the British Museum Sloane Ms. for the Epidemiological Society of London XI-XII William Boghurst Shaw, 1894

Ancestry's Red Book, American State, County & Town Sources. Eicholz, Alice, PHD 1992

An address on the study of race, to the Anthropology Association of 1962, annual meeting published in the year book annals of the Encyclopedia Americana 1964

An Address to The Whites Speech Delivered in the First Presbyterian Church Philadelphia, MAY 26, 1826 by Elias Boudinot, Excerpted by the National Humanities Center for use in a Professional Development Seminar

A New and full, critical, biographical, and geographical history of Scotland: containing the history of the succession of their kings from Robert Bruce, to the present time. With a geographical description of the several counties... together with an appendix... and a map of each county in Scotland, William Duff Printed for the author, 1749

A New Collection of Voyages, Discoveries and Travels: Containing Whatever is Worthy of Notice, in Europe, Asia, Africa and America, Volume 5 by John Knox J. Knox, 1767

A New Geography for Children by Harriet Beecher Stowe Sampson Low, 1855

A new voyage to Italy: with curious observations on several other countries, as: Germany, Switzerland, Savoy, Geneva, Flanders, and Holland; together with useful instructions for those who shall travel thither, Volume 1, Part 1 Maximilien Misson Printed for R. Bonwicke, 1714

Angelo Soliman-Friend of Mozart. Vol 7 No1 Nettl, Paul Clark Atlanta University 1946

A Philosophical and Political History of the British Settlements and trade in North America: by Abbe Raynal in two volumes. Vol II. EDINBURGH:

A Pictorial History of Black Americans, 5th revised edition by Langston Hughes, Milton Meltzer, and C. Eric Lincoln. Crown Publishers New York 1983

A Short Account of the Plague: Or Malignant fever, lately Prevalent in Philadephia: with a Statement on the proceedings that Took place in different parts of the United States. Mathew Carey 1794

A Short View of the Families of the Scottish Nobility: Their Titles, Marriages, Issue, Descents; To which are Added, a List of All Those Peers Who Have Served in Parliament Since the Union; By Mr. Salmon by Nathaniel Salmon W. Owen, 1759

A Strange Case of Mistaken Identity: Mapp, Alf J. Madison Books NY, London 1987

A Study of history by Arnold Toynbee. Abridgement of volumes I-VI Oxford University Press New York and London. 1946

A wizard's wandering from China to Peru. By John Watkins Holden FSS 1885

African Kingdoms, Davidson, Basil: Time Life Books Collection The Great Ages of Man. 1978

A History of English Speaking Peoples. Churchill, Winston The New World, Bantam Books INC New York 1956

An Universal History: From the Earliest Accounts to the Present Time, Part 1, Volume 16 George Sale, George Psalmanazar, Archibald Bower, George Shelvocke, John Campbell, John Swinton C. Bathurst, Princeton University 1780

A Social History of Black slaves in and freedmen in Portugal, 1441-1555 A. C. DE. C. M Saunders NY: Cambridge University Press 1982

Auschwitz, 1270 to the Present. Dwork, Deborah & Robert Jan Pelt. W. W. Norton & Company, 1996
BBC News. Mali conflict: Timbuktu manuscripts destroyed 6/28/2015 http://www.bbc.com/news/world

Between the World and Me Coates, Ta-Nahesi 2015

Blacks, Reds, and Russians: Sojourners in Search of the Soviet Promise by Carew, Joy Gleason Rutgers University Press, 2010

Britain Life World Library by John Oshborne NY 1961

Chronicle of the Kings of England: With Additions Richard Baker 1670

Democracy Matters Winning the Fight Against Imperialism. West, Cornel Penguin Press New York 2004

Department of Interior, Census Office Compendium of the Eleventh Census 1890 Part I-Population. Robert P. Porter Superintendent. Washington D.C. Government Printing Office 1892.

Description of Africa: Olfert Dapper, Nauwkeurige Beschrijvinge der Afrikaansche Gewesten 1668

Early schools & school-books of New England: George Emery Littlefield, The Club of Odd Vols, 1545

Ebony magazine How Negroes live in Russia. Davis, William January 1960

Emil Gassner, ed., Im Dienste Europas: Funf Jahre deutscher Arbeit in General gouvernment Cracow: Zeitungsverlag Krakrau-Warschau, 1944, 31

England's Battles with the Boers in the Transvaal, Including an Exhaustive History of the Settlement of Cape Colony, Wars with the Kaffirs, Matabeles, Zulus, the Diamond and Gold Mines of South Africa and a History of Exploration, Discovery, Conquest and Development by All the Famous Travelers that Have Traversed the Dark Continent ... James William Buel Fighting in Africa:

103

Eugene Onegin, Chapter 1 stanza 50, Pushkin, Aleksandr

Exploring African law and ancient Egypt Hensley, Travis Doctoral research: loc blog August 2017

Fallen founder, the life of Aaron Burr Viking Nancy Isenberg

Fiesco or, The Genoese Conspiracy, A Tragedy, Friedrich Schiller

Freedom on My Mind: A History of African Americans, with Documents. Vol. 2. White, Deborah G., Mia Bay, and Waldo E. Martin. Bedford, 2013.

From Hunters to Farmers: The Causes and Consequences of Food Production in Africa. John Desmond Clark, Steven A. Brandt. University of California Press, Jan 1, 1984
Guns Germs and Steel

Hartford Courant, "Jews in Russia" October 21, 1915. Washington Oct 17

Hartford in the olden time: its first thirty years, by Scæva, ed. by W.M.B. Hartley 1853

Heritage of World Civilizations: Pearson,

Histoire des États-Unis by Grégoire Jeanne C.F. Chamerot, 1894

History for Ready Reference: From the Best Historians, Biographers, and Specialists; Their Own Words in a Complete System of History. Larned, Josephus Nelson and Alan Campbell Riley C.A. Nichols Company, 1910.

History of Herodotus, Volume 1 page 121 Herodotus Halicarnasseus, George Rawlinson, Henry Creswicke Rawlinson (sir), John Gardner Wilkinson

History of Middlesex County, Connecticut: With Biographical Sketches of Its Prominent Men. J.B. Beers & Company, 1884

History of the United States of America: 1861-1865. The civil war James Scholler Dodd, Mead, 1899

History of the wars, Books III and IV (Vandalic War) Translated by, Harvard University Press, Procopius

http://www.britannica.com/EBchecked/topic/457164/Phoenician-languageTuareg accessed February 4th, 2015
http://www.metmuseum.org/toah/hd/wax/hdwax.htm accessed 2/4/15
http://www.pbs.org/wgbh/pages/frontline/shows/secret/famous/royalfamily.htmlIN
Illustrated Atlas of world History. Simon Adams, John Briquebec, Ann Kramer. 1992

In Answer to a Book Intittled Elkon Basilike, the Portraiture of his Sacred Majesty in his Solitudes and Sufferings Milton, John, Kearsley, G, Eikonoklastes: 1770

International Military Tribunal, Nuremberg. "Document # USSR-40 (Exhibit # USSR 40)" 1946

Journal of Ancient Egyptian Interconnections. Schneider, Thomas University of Arizona online 2011

Journal of the American Geographical Society of New York, Volume 17 The Society, 1885

Journey into the Whirlwind, Ginsburg, Eugenia Houghton Mifflin Harcourt, Nov 4, 2002

Kipling, Rudyard: Letters of Travel, Garden City New York. Doubleday, Page & Co. 1920

Know the 56 signers of the Declaration of Independence by George Ross. Rand McNally 1963

Lafayette a life 1936 by Andreas latzko translated from German by E. W. Dickens

Leo (Africanus), Robert Brown, John Pory Hakluyt Society, 1896 pg. 859

Letters of Thomas Jefferson

Letters to a Young Gentleman Commencing His Education: With a Brief History of the United States by Noah Webster Howe & Spalding, S. Converse, printer, 1823 received by Harvard College in 1879.

Literary History of the United States, 3rd ED Spiller, Robert etal 1963

Long road to liberty, Oklahoma's African American history and Culture Oklahoma Tourism and recreation department. Oklahoma City OK.

Loose papers: or facts gathered during eight years residence in Ireland, Scotland, England, France and Germany. Nicholson, Asenath 1853

Mein Kampf: My Struggle: (Vol. I & Vol. II) - eKitap Projesi, Hitler, Adolf. Jan 31, 2016

Memoirs 1925-1950 George F Kennan An Atlantic Monthly Press Bk 1967

Memoirs of Governor William Smith, of Virginia: His Political, Military, and Personal History by John W. Bell, William Smith Moss engraving Company, 1891

Modern History or the Present State of All Nations, Volume 2 Thomas Salmon 1745

Morgenthau, Henry (1918). Ambassador Morgenthau's Story. Garden City, New York: Doubleday.

Moscow, St Petersburg and the Golden Ring 2nd Edition Nordbye, Masha.

Mysteries of History by Robert Stewart National Geographic Washington DC 2003

Narrative of Travels and Discoveries in Northern and Central Africa, in the Years 1822,1823, and 1824, by Major Denham, Captain Clapperton, and the Late Doctor Oudney, Published by Authority of the Right Honourable Earl Bathurst.

Nations Beyond the Seas, Wallace, Atwood and Helen Goss Thomas 1930

NATIVES. (1804, September 2). The Sydney Gazette and New South Wales Advertiser (NSW:1803 - 1842), p. 2. Retrieved March 9, 2015, from http://nla.gov.au/nla.news-article626394

Nazi Conspiracy and Aggression, (Volume 4) United States. Office of Chief of Counsel for the Prosecution of Axis Criminality U.S. Government Printing Office, 1946

New Perspectives in World History. 34th year book of the National Council for the Social Studies. Engle, Shirley 1964

Observations on the Antiquities Historical and Monumental of the County of Cornwall (etc.)-Oxford, W. Jackson 1754 by William Borlase (Cornish English vocabulary)

Oliver Cromwell Popular History. Rev. M. Russell. D. M. Mac Lelland Book Co. New York 1910

Outlines of German Literature Joseph Gostwick & Robert Harrison Holt & Williams F. W Christern 1873

Oxford Universal dictionary reprinted with Addenda in 1955

Past Worlds The times atlas of Archaeology. Chris Scarre, Guild Publishing London 1988

Peasant Rebels Under Stalin: Collectivization and the Culture of Peasant Resistance. Viola, Lynne. Oxford University Press, Jan 28, 1999

Poems on the affairs of the state in the time of Oliver Cromwell.

Proceedings in the Senate and House of Representatives Upon the Reception and Acceptance from the State of Maryland of the Statues of Charles Carroll of Carrollton and of John Hanson, Erected in Statuary Hall of the Capitol: January 31, 1903 United States. Congress U.S. Government Printing Office, 1903

Publications Relative to the Difference of Opinion Between the Governor and the Council [of Maryland] on Their Respective Powers by Alexander Contee Hanson Frederick Green, Printer to the State, 1803

Quarterly of the California Historical Society Vol VII No.2 L Leidesdorff-Folsome estate June 1928

Reclaiming the Ancient Manuscripts of Timbuktu by Chris Rainier for National Geographic News May 27, 2003

Redemption Song Bob Marely.

Report and Resolutions of State Officers, Board and Committees to the General Assembly of the State of South Carolina. Volume II South Carolina, General Assembly 1891

Russian Foreign Policy Essays in Historical Perspective New Haven and London University Press. Lederer, Ivo J. (as represented by R.A. Fadeev's Opinion on the Eastern Question and N. Ia. Danilevskii's Russia and Europe published in 1869)

New York Times Special. "Feds are working among Negroes." Widespread Propaganda by Radical Leaders Known to the Government. New York Times October 19, 1919

New York Times Special. Lucon Assails New Law: Says Attempts to De Christianize the world has begun in France. New York Times Feb 4, 1925

New York Times. Fall in Birth Rates Aids Peace of Europe. Callender, Harold. March 18, 1928

Speeches of John Philpot Curran, Esq: With the Speeches of Grattan, Erskine and Burke. To which is Prefixed, A Brief Sketch of the History of Ireland, and Also a Biographical Account of Mr. Curran, Vol 1 John Philpot Curran, Henry Grattan, Thomas Erskine Baron Erskine, Edmund Burke I. Riley, 1809

Stalin's Genocides, Naimark, Norman M. Princeton University Press, Dec 25, 2011

State Historical Society of North Dakota, Collections, Volume 1 1906

The Age of Napoleon: The Story of Civilization By Will Durant, Ariel Durant

The Auschwitz Volunteer: Beyond Bravery: Pilecki, Witold Jarek Garlinski Trade select Ltd, 2012

The Autobiography of Benjamin Franklin Art Type Edition. The world's popular classic Books Inc. NY.

The Bible Through the ages. Reader's Digest Association Pleasanville NY Montreal 1996

The Boy Travellers in the Land of the Czar. Kingston, William Henry, G. Fred Markham in Russia: Or, Griffith and Farran, 1858

The Cambridge History of Africa, Volume 2 J. D. Fage, Roland Anthony Oliver, Cambridge University

Press, 1978

The Chief Culprit: Stalin's Grand Design to Start World War II. Suvorov, Viktor. Naval Institute Press, Feb 18, 2013

The Circassian chief. Kingston, William Henry G. 1843

The Club of Odd Volumes, 1545

The Columbia Encyclopedia. Columbia University Press. 3rd Edition 1963

The Cruise Steam Yacht North Star: England, Russia, Denmark, France, Spain, Italy, ' Malta, Turkey, Madeira, ETC. REV. John Overton Choules, D.D.: James Blackwood, Paternoster Row. London 1854.

The Dealings of God, Man and the Devil: As Exemplified in the Life, Experience, and Travels of Lorenzo Dow, in a Period of Over Half a Century, Volume 2 Dow, Lorenzo. Nafia & Cornish, 1850.

The Devil's Race Track: Mark Twain's Great Dark Writings: the best From which was the Dream and the Fables of Man... Tuckey, John and Watson, Richard: University of California Press, 1980

The Encyclopædia Britannica: A-ZYM Day Otis Kellogg, Thomas Spencer Baynes, William Robertson Smith Werner, 1903 volume(F)Fezzan pg. 129-130

The Etymology of Cornish surnames, Patronymica Cornu-Britannica: or, by Richard Stephen Charnock Longmans, Green, Reader and Dyer, 1870

The Favorite Works of Mark Twain Twain, Mark Garden City Publishing Co. INC 1939

The Founding Fathers, Benjamin Franklin in His Own Words. Thomas Fleming Newsweek NY 1972

The Grove Encyclopedia of Islamic Art and Architecture, Volume 3 Jonathan M. Bloom, Sheila Blair Oxford University Press, 2009 – Art

The Gulf of the Red Sea. Pliny

The Historical Library of Diodorus the Sicilian: In Fifteen Books. To which are Added the Fragments of Diodorus, and Those Published by H. Valesius, I. Rhodomannus, & F. Ursinus, translated by G Booth ESQ Harvard College Library In two volumes. Vol. 1 byDiodorus (Siculus.) Harvard College Library In two volumes. Vol. 1 printed by W.M Dowall 1814

The History and Description of Africa: And of the Notable Things Therein Contained by Leo (Africanus), Robert Brown, John Pory Hakluyt Society, 1896 pg. 776

The History of England, Volume 1 Rapin de Thoyras (Paul, M.) J. and P. Knapton, 1743

The History of Scotland, from the year 1423 until the year 1542: Containing the lives and reigns of James the I. the to the V. With several memorials of state, during the reigns of James VI. and Charles V. William Drummond Tomlins and himself, 1655

The History of the Revolutions in the Empire of Morocco: Upon the Death of the Late Emperor Muley Ishmael; Being a Most Exact Journal of what Happen'd in Those Parts in the Last and Part of the Present Year. With Observations Natural, Moral and Political, Relating to that Country and People. By John Braithwaite, James and John Knapton, Arthur Bettesworth, 1729

The History of the Works of the Learned, or an Impartial account of Books lately printed in all parts of Europe, Volume 9 by H. Rhodes, 1707 The commission of Cosma of Egypt's Christian Typography.

The Intelligence Officer's Bookshelf Studies in Intelligence Vol.53, No 3 compiled and reviewed by CIA B. Peake Hayden, (Extracts, September 2010)

The Jeffersonian Cyclopedia: A Comprehensive Collection of the Views of Thomas Jefferson Classified and Arranged in Alphabetical Order Under Nine Thousand Titles Relating to Government, Politics, Law, Education, Political Economy, Finance, Science, Art, Literature, Religious Freedom, Morals, Etc by Thomas Jefferson Funk & Wagnalls Company, 1900 page

The Jews and Moors in Spain by Joseph Krauskopf M. Berkowitz & Company, 1886. This is the best account of the history of Spain and the invasion from the records of Arabians and the comprehensive research of this author. P228

The Journal of Egyptian Archaeology. Vol. 84, 1998 Gnomons at Meroë and Early Trigonometry.

The Journey-book of England. Berkshire (Derbyshire, Hampshire, Kent). By England 1840

The Knickerbocker; Or, New-York Monthly Magazine, Volume 42 1853 pg. 263

The Letters of F. Scott Fitzgerald (New York Charles Scribner's Sons, 1963) accessed from Le Vot, Andre F. Scott Fitzgerald a Biography 1983

The Life of Alfred the Great Reinhold Pauli, Paulus Orosius, Benjamin Thorpe, G. Bell & sons, 1893 World history

The life of Friedrich Schiller comprehending an examination of his works. Thomas Carlyle, Dana Estes and Co. Boston 1825

The Marcus Garvey and United Negro Improvement Association Papers, Volume XII: The Caribbean Diaspora, 1920-1921, Volume 12 Garvey, Marcus Duke University Press, 2014

The Negro Church in America by E. Franklin Frazier, Schocken Books. New York. 1968

The Negro in the American Revolution chapel hill Benjamin Quarles, pg.198 (from Connecticut Black Soldiers 1775-1783 by David White 1973. Pequot Press Chester Connecticut.)

The New Jim Crow: Mass Incarceration in the Age of Colorblindness. Alexander, Michelle The New Press, 2013

The New Larned History for Ready Reference, Reading and Research: The Actual Words of the World's Best Historians, Volume 1 Josephus Nelson Larned 1524

The New York Herald-Tribune: "Alleged Red Plot to convert Negroes into Bolshevists." New York, June 28 –(AP)– June 29, 1927 HC

The New York Times Traveler, By William S. Niederkorn, 8/12,1909

The Origins and Consequences of Stalinism. Medvedev, Roy A. and George Shriver. Let History Judge: Columbia University Press, 1989

The Peerage of Ireland: A Genealogical and Historical Account of All the Peers of that Kingdom; Their Descents, Collateral Branches, Births, Marriages, and Issue ... with Paternal Coats of Arms, Crests, Supporters, and Mottoes ... Some Account of the Antient Kings, &c, Volume 2 by Edward Kimber, John Almon, 1768 pages 4,121,179, 210.

The Planters Plea, or The Grounds of Plantations Examined..." [London 1630], in Force, ed., Tracts. II, 19-20, 45" Diamond, Sigmund, Sellers, Charles. The creation of society in the New World. The Berkeley Series in American History The recruitment of a population Chapter III White, John.

The Present State Of Music In Germany, The Netherlands, And United Provinces. Or The Journal of a Tour Through Those Countries, Undertaken to Collect Materials for A General History Of Music: In Two Volumes, Volume 2 Charles Burney, Becket, 1775

The Presidents of the United States, White House Historical Association: Freidel, Franklin

The Rise of the Spanish Empire in the Old World and in the New, Volume 1 by Roger Bigelow Merriman Macmillan, 1918 page 14-23

The Song of Roland: Done Into English, in the Original Measure Dutton, 1920 Pg. 63

The source book of medieval history: documents illustrative of European life and institutions from the German invasion to the Renaissance by Frederic Austin 1908

The Story of Africa and its Explorers, Robert Brown 1896

The story of a throne Catherine ii of Russia

The United States in 1800 by Henry Adams, Man and Society Vol. 6 Gateway to great Books 1963

The War on Prohibition and the rise of the American State. Lisa MC

The White Slaves of England compiled from Official documents with twelve spirited illustrations by James Cobden, Miller, Orton & Mulligan, 1853

The Workers in American History: by James Oneal, National Rip-Saw 1912

The Works of Lord Byron Canton XII Don Juan (2) Malthus

The works of Nicholas Machiavelli, Machiavelli, Nicholas

The Works of Washington Irving volume 5 The New Hudson Edition P.F. Collier and son NY

The works of William Shakespeare, by Alexander Pope 1861 volume 1

The World An Illustrated History edited by Geoffrey Parker Harper row publishers New York 1986

The Youth's History of the United States Vol I by, Edward. Ellis A.M New York 1887

Thomas Jefferson an intimate history by Fawn H Brodie 1974

Thomas Jefferson, A Strange Case of Mistaken Identity by Alf J Mapp Jr. Madison Books 1987

Three "Whys" of the Russian Revolution. Pipes, Richard Vintage Books Division of Random House New York. 1995

Timbuctoo the Mysteries. Felix DuBois 1897

Titus Livius Patavinus, by Giacomo Filippo Tomasini, Andreas Frisius, 1670

Travels in North America in the years 1780-82, Marquis de Chastellux Howard Rice pg229 (Chapel Hill 1963)(from Connecticut Black Soldiers 1775-1783 by David White 1973. Pequot Press Chester Connecticut.)

Travels in Syria and Egypt, During the Years 1783, 1784, & 1785, Volume 1 Constantin-François Volney R. Morison, 1801 p. 55. NOW by Joel A. Freeman, Ph.D.

Treasures & Traditions. Smithsonian Institution, Travelling Exhibit Service. Washington D.C 1990

Two Thousand Years of Gild Life: An Outline of the History and Development of the Gild System from Early Times, with Special Reference to Its Application to Trade and Industry; Together with a Full Account of the Gilds and Trading Companies of Kingston-upon-Hull, from the 14th to the 18th Century Joseph Malet Lambert A. Brown and sons; [etc., etc.,], 1891

Under the Sky of My Africa: Alexander Pushkin and Blackness. Nepomnyashchy, Catharine Theimer, Nicole Svobodny, Ludmilla A. Trigos Northwestern University Press, May 30, 2006

United States Congress. House. Committee on the Judiciary. Hearings Before the Committee on the Judiciary, House of Representatives, Sixty-sixth Congress, First[-third] Session U.S. Government Printing Office, 1919

University of Minnesota pamphlets on American writers no. 57 Jack London page 12 by Charles Walcutt 1966 North Central publishing co St. Paul

Vergennes letters to Thomas Jefferson. 3/18/1786

Violence, The Klu Klux Klan and the struggle for equality. An informational and instructional kit. The Connecticut Education Association, The council on interracial Books for children and the National Education Association. May 1981

Webster's new explorer desk encyclopedia 2003 Musa Emperor of Mali from 1307/ 1324

Webster's New International Dictionary of the English Language Based on the International Dictionary of 1890 and 1900: Now Completely Revised in All Departments, Including Also a Dictionary of Geography and Biography, Being the Latest Authentic Quarto Edition of the Merriam Series, Volume 1. G. & C. Merriam Company, 1926

We hold these truths, Catholic Reflections on the American proposition. John Courtney Murray, S.J Sheed and Ward INC 1960

Women's Home Missions of the Methodist Episcopal Church Women's Home Missionary Society of the Methodist Church vl 37-38 1920

World Revolution The Plot Against Civilization, Webster, Nesta Small, Maynard & Co Publishers Boston

Woodrow Wilson as I Know Him. Tumulty, Joseph P. Garden City, NY: Doubleday, 1921.

Yankee Doodle, Green, pp. 118-19p57: The history of ancient Windsor, Connecticut, New York 1859 pp879 (from Connecticut Black Soldiers 1775-1783 by David White 1973. Pequot Press Chester Connecticut)

Zanzibar: Its History and Its People W.H. Ingrams.

Table of Events

- 1783   British forced to recognize American Independence
- 1784   Serfdom Abolished in Denmark
- 1784   Thomas Jefferson Land Ordinance
- 1789   French Revolution third estate declares itself the national assembly
- ....   feudal system abolished. Royalist begin to flee
- ....   Radicheft journeys to Moscow to plead for the emancipation of Slavs
- 1790   first Penitentiary built in PA
- 1790   Haitians defeat Napoleon forces
- 1793   Royal Vendee in France revolt against national reforms
- 1792   US government divided between two parties' republican under Jefferson and Federalist
- ....   under Hamilton & Adams
- 1792   Catholicism banned in France
- 177
- 1792   AME church erected in PA
- 1794   Polish general Kosciusko defeated, moves to Chicago & leaves President Thomas ....
  Jefferson as executor of his estate, to ensure the education of Blacks
- 1797   first copper pennies and pound notes produced in England
- 1800   Gabriel Prosser leads unsuccessful uprising against Thomas Jefferson administration
- 1800   Thomas Jefferson President of US primary 80% of revenue is from custom receipts
- 1801   T.J begins war with Barbary States
- 1803   Thomas Jefferson administration gives French money to finance their government
  reforms with from Louisiana purchase
- 1804   All States North of Maryland have abolished slavery
- 1806   British take Cape of Good hope and major cotton industry in South Africa.
- 1808   Thomas Jefferson prohibits the immigration of Negros
- 1812   Louisiana becomes a state
- 1812   Great Moscow burned
- 1813   Toronto burned
- 1813   last gold Guinea coins issued in England
- 1814   Washington burned along with the Library of Congress
- 1816   African Methodist Episcopal Church AME
- 1816   American colonization society begins process to send Blacks to Africa
- 1816   first Prison built as model for US prison system. NY
- 1816   Indiana becomes a state
- 1817   Mississippi becomes a state
- 1818   Illinois becomes a state
- 1819   Alabama becomes a state
- 1821   African Methodist Episcopal Church AME
- 1822   The Phoenix Society New York
- 1827   Freedom Journal
- 1830   France captures Algiers
- 1831   The term underground railroad used
- 1836   Henry Blair cotton Planter
- 1837   Elijah Lovejoy Killed and his printing of office in Illinois burnt.
- 1837   Michigan becomes a state
- 1837   Earliest official birth records available for England
- 1838   Alexander Twiglight Vermont Legislature
- 1839   Amistad seized in New England carrying 54 passengers from Africa to Louisiana.
- 1841   USS Creole seized and turned away from Louisiana sails to Bahamas
- 1844   Several city blocks burned in the Irish dominated suburbs of Kensington PA
- 1845   James P. Beckworth discovers shortcut through the Sierra Nevada and gold in California.
- 1846   1 million killed off in Ireland Famine (attorney John Curran refers to the victims as the
- ....   "Western Negroes" and pleads with the British government for help.
- 1848   Frederick Douglas Publishes the North Star
- 1848   Horatio King builds Alabama's first bridge
- 1848   Serfdom Abolished in Austria
- 1850   California gold rush leads to California becoming a state
- 1850   50K Africans move to Cuba and Brazil per year

- 1850   Opens the flood gates to Whites while enslaving blacks
- 1854   Lincoln University
- 1857   US supreme court rules slavery legal in Dread Scott trial
- 1862   Confederate ships commandeered by Blacks, sails
- 1863   New York destroyed by fire and 1,200 dead
- 1865   American Civil War
- 1866   Austria expelled from German Confederation Vienna divided Reds against Blacks.
- 1866   <u>KKK established</u>
- 1867   US government gives Russia 7.2 million to begin their revolution
- 1867   Records of early American government and Ben Franklin Bio first surface.
- 1869   Continental Railroad completed
- 1870   Library of Strasbourg burned
- 1871   Louvre and other public buildings burned
- 1871   Chicago burned
- 1872   Thomas J Martin discovers technology to invent the fire extinguisher
- 1872   Mc Coy invents self-lubricating engine for railroad industry
- 1876   Ole Erekson creates official portraits of original leaders of US government.
- 1876   P.B.S of Louisiana denied seat in congress
- 1880   Alexander Ashbourne oil refinery
- 1884   Boghurst Shaw publishes an account of the plague of 1666
- 1891   Daniel Hale founds provident Hospital in Chicago and performs first open-heart surgery
- 1891   JA Lester National Medical Association Tennesse
- 1892   First ever medical journal started in US by Miles Vandahurst Lynk Tennesse
- 1893   Granville Woods company provides many improvements to rail way systems
- 1898   North Carolina Mutual Life founded
- 1902   Maggie Lena Walker (1864-1934) establishes the Penny Savings Bank of Virginia
- 1906   Atlanta under attack, massive destruction
- 1912   Titanic sank
- 1916   Anthony B Crawford lynched
- 1916-   US occupation of Hispaniola during WWI.
- 1917   East St. Louis burned
- 07/1919   Washington fire
- 08/1919   Knoxville Tennessee fire
- 08/1919   Chicago fire cripples' city
- 1920   Elijah McCoy Manufacturing company established
- 1920   Elijah McCoy and wife hit in major car accident, both die within a few years (NO heirs)
- 1920   Rosewood Florida burned
- 1921   Black Wall St in Tulsa OK burned
- 1922   Public records office of Ireland burned.
- 1924   Mathew Henson is the first American to reach North Pole, but Peary, a White man
  ....   receives the medal of honor.
    1926   Carter Woodson establishes Black History Month
- 1927   Castries St. Lucia burned records destroyed.
- 1930s   Dr. Charles Drew invents method for storing blood. Pioneers Red Cross Blood Banking
- 1937   Blacks massacred from Western Hispaniola.
              Island divided into two nations Haiti and Dominican Republic.
- 1948   Castries St. Lucia burned and ship in harbor bombed by Germans. Records destroyed
- 1950   Dr. Charles Drew, killed in car accident.
- 2008-   The world in the form of a Jeffersonian story ends, When Barack Obama is elected for
  2016   two terms as president of the United States.

Nigga, Naygur, Negus, Nigger

---

[i] The word is also spelled Naygur in Rudyard Kipling's Departmental Ditties. Pronounced by an Irishman. "Tis a no-good policy to swindle the Naygur av his hard-earned emolument's."
Departmental Ditties Rudyard Kipling Homewood Publishing Co. Chicago 1902) 86-101

Made in the USA
Middletown, DE
09 February 2023

24439450R00064